Alba

43 W

Chicago

Kildare 8657

DATE DUE

JE 4'98			

OLIVER CROMWELL

A STUDY IN PERSONAL RELIGION

OLIVER CROMWELL

A STUDY IN PERSONAL RELIGION

BY

ROBERT F. HORTON, M.A., D.D.

AUTHOR OF

'JOHN HOWE,' 'THE TEACHING OF JESUS,' 'THE ART OF LIVING
TOGETHER,' ETC.

NEW YORK

THOMAS WHITTAKER

2 & 3 BIBLE HOUSE

1897

DEDICATION

TO THE YOUNG FREE CHURCHMEN
OF ENGLAND

Though wreaths from adult hands be all unseized,
Our crowns are crowns indeed if thrown by you.

SUFFER me to dedicate this book to you. If you will
give it your attention and absorb its lesson, I shall be
well content, though every one else should mislike or
condemn it. England has grudged you the knowledge
of your hero. By slander and hatred and ignorance she
has tried to make you suspect or forget Oliver Cromwell ;
and yet, as she needs you, you need him. Yes, England
needs you. She addresses you with scornful lips and
averts her eyes from you, but she needs you. She needed
Cromwell and she treated him in the same way. In her
great heart she knows—sometimes in moments of humility
she owns—that to you and your fathers she owes almost
all that is best in her, and that if you and your sons
should disappear from her borders her day would decline.
She feigns not to love you, but she needs you.

And you need Cromwell. He is the man of the hour
for you. Your work for England and the world, if it is
to be done, must be done precisely as he did his. The
spirit in which he wrought has no precise parallel in
history. But that is the spirit in which you have to

work. Through the same odium and misrepresentation, accumulated plots, conspiracies, derision, and dread, you must pass. Your throne, like his, will be one of duty not of delight. Your recognition, like his, may have to wait for centuries, for millenniums.

My young brothers—and sisters too—as I know you, the young life of the Free Churches of England, my heart goes out to you ; you have a good purpose, and your task is to realise in England some of the grand and sweet ideals which were in Oliver's brain. His great, orderly, godly state, religious, tolerant, powerful, is yet to be. You have to toil for it. Your contemporaries are for the most part working in quite another direction. Charles and Laud are the hero and saint of the day. But wait awhile. Your Cromwell is at hand. His banner is not obscurely unfurled. And for the present I hear him writing from Huntingdon (the words were written on August 2, 1643): "I understand the good affections of your young men and maids, for which God is to be praised. . . . I thank God for stirring up the youth to cast in their mite, which I desire may be employed to the best advantage . . . and rest, your loving friend, Oliver Cromwell."

For the work of the Church and of the State practically everything depends on the "good affections of the young men and the maids," and I would readily lay down my life to think that you had read and assimilated this little book of mine. With prayers for your well-being, I rest your loving friend,

ROBERT F. HORTON.

HAMPSTEAD, 5th January 1897.

PROEM

In the National Portrait Gallery, between the chamber
which contains the elegant but somewhat vapid figures
of Charles I. and his courtiers, and the chamber which
contains the rollicking and sensual figures of the court of
Charles II., there is a narrow room filled with portraits,
grave of countenance, sober in attire, and lit with a
strange spiritual gleam in their eyes—these are the men
of the Commonwealth. Henry Ireton, the political
idealist and intrepid dreamer of constitutional dreams;
Lambert, with the grace and gentleness of an inspired
preacher and the undaunted courage of a hero; Thurloe,
Whitlocke, Vane, and Walker, the gifted painter of
Oliver and of the others—Walker did for the Commonwealth what Van Dyck did for Charles I. and Dobson for
Charles II.—and Oliver himself, over the likeness of
Milton which represents him as the twin-spirit of Oliver.
They have a character all their own. Their like will be
found in the future of England rather than in intervening
centuries. Oliver, not beautiful to look on, is benignant,
firm, modest, a high-erected type of man, less refined,
more forceful than the others, but obviously a religious
man; a man, one would say at once, whose religion must
be understood before he can be; a man who will warn off
both portrait painter and biographer who cannot enter
into this which is the spring and impulse of his life.
A religious period in the history of England! The
most profoundly and consistently religious spirit of the
period!

INTRODUCTORY SONNET

You ask me for a charm against disease—
Not of the body (you can bow to that),
But of the spirit, which you tremble at,
Lest it should dull your fine-wrought sympathies
With vigorous human life, and slowly freeze
The sinews of your mind, till they grow dumb
As the dead limbs they live with, and become
Useless for all high purposes like these.
What is my counsel?
                    Choose a hero.
                                    Then
Make him your study—temper, brain, and nerve,
Till he has grown your stronger self.   And when
Weak, morbid impulse comes on you to swerve
From the sane path, his gifted strength shall serve
To keep you true to God, your soul, and men.

EDWARD CRACROFT LEFROY'S
Sonnet to an Invalid.

CONTENTS

OLIVER CROMWELL

A STUDY IN PERSONAL RELIGION

CHAPTER I

THE TASK AND THE MAN

1599–1642

"The memory of Oliver Cromwell, as I count, has a good many centuries in it."—CARLYLE.

DURING his lifetime the greatest man of the age, 1599 for two hundred years after his death overwhelmed with infamy as a hypocrite and a usurper, then discovered, vindicated, and set among the greatest names of all ages, Oliver Cromwell furnishes a curious and fascinating subject of study.

"The collection of all his speeches, letters, and sermons," said Hume, "would make a great curiosity, and, with a few exceptions, might pass for one of the most nonsensical books in the world."

This collection Thomas Carlyle laboriously made
and gave to the world in December 1845.
And it certainly did "make a great curiosity,"
but instead of being, as Hume anticipated, one of
the most nonsensical books in the world, it has
seemed to some serious readers for these last
fifty years one of the bravest, sincerest, and most
inspiring books in the world, and bids fair to
stand tolerably secure when all Hume's historical
writings are forgotten.

But in spite of Carlyle's splendid service to
a maligned hero, and in spite of the several
biographies which have been prompted by the
Letters and Speeches, something has yet to be
done before Cromwell can be properly understood.
On the whole the best biography of him lies
scattered over the pages of Professor S. R.
Gardiner's *History of England*, *History of the
Great Civil War*, and *History of the Commonwealth and the Protectorate*, the three great works
which have at last admitted the quiet and impartial
light of truth into the troubled period that lies
between 1603 and 1660. The additional facts
which Professor Gardiner has discovered, and the
corrections which he has been able to make in
even Carlyle's diligent work, are the justification

for attempting to tell the story of Cromwell's life again. But even this is not the reason for the present book. The present book asks to be read on another ground, which should be stated at once.

Cromwell was not only a religious man, he was a man to whom his religion was everything. To understand him, it is necessary to understand his religion and to sympathise with it. His life, which makes an impression on the world simply as a factor in the politics of the time, was to him a piece of work wrought under the great Taskmaster's eye, which could only be judged in relation to eternity. Now even Professor Gardiner, writing not as a biographer but as a historian, is compelled to regard Oliver Cromwell principally as a soldier and a statesman playing a remarkable part in the history of his country. He is only able to drop occasional *obiter dicta* on the subject which to Cromwell himself was the all-important consideration of his life. That subject is, it is true, sufficiently clear in Carlyle's book, because it glows and throbs in almost everything which Cromwell either spoke or wrote. But Carlyle was hardly in a position to make a study of Cromwell as a Christian and an Independent. And strange

to say, the later biographers have been either men
who had no special sympathy with the Independent
standpoint in religion, or men who have definitely
broken with the Christian faith.   They no more
than Carlyle have been in a position to develop
the life from its central idea, which was the
passionate Puritan creed, or to exhibit it,—and
this was how it appeared to Cromwell himself,—
as a work of the Divine Spirit carried out by an
imperfect but desperately sincere man.[1]

It is entirely from this point of view that we
are now to consider the life.   That adventurous
career will be sketched as fully as the narrow space
allows, but it will be sketched avowedly from the
inside, that is, as it appeared to the chief actor
himself.   There will be no attempt made to
eulogise his achievements; the narration of them
is their best eulogy.   There will be no attempt to

---

[1] Mr. Frederic Harrison, in the *Twelve English
Statesmen* series, does his best to fairly apprehend the
faith and experience which are at the centre of Cromwell's
life ; but he has, at the outset (p. 27), to confess that he
and his sympathisers are in this matter outsiders, though,
he touchingly adds, "we are the dear friends, children,
parents, brothers, and sisters of those who live by the
Gospel alone."   It is a great literary feat to have written
so good a life of Cromwell with so radical a disqualification
for the task.

excuse what are called his "crimes." As they are described from his standpoint, and set in the circumstances which occasioned them, they are seen not to be crimes at all, but that kind of masterful action which in an age of callous feeling and of political upheaval, in the execution of a vast and almost unparalleled task, we must be prepared to expect, unless the workman is raised above all human infirmities. Oliver Cromwell was subject to like passions with ourselves. He had great faults—that is to say, he was human. He made great blunders which it is not difficult for us to discover and censure. But he was equal to his task, and considering what that task was, of whom else could so much be said?

Now, viewing the man's life as a plan of God, and the man as an instrument raised up to accomplish a certain object for England and for religion, let us ask what was the task which required doing? Briefly it was this : The power of an ancient throne had to be limited, and in order to be limited, it had first to be broken ; the principle of religious liberty had to be brought from the region of abstract speculation, in which it had been born, into the field of practical politics, where it had no existence. The English monarchy, which from its origin in

Saxon times had never been entirely divorced from the principle of national control, had, after the Wars of the Roses and the ruin of the old nobility, been transformed into an autocracy, moderated at first by that shrewd sense of the national prejudices which never quite forsook the Tudors. But when the great English queen was gone, the Stuarts inherited the Tudor ideas of personal government without any of their tact in feeling the pulse of England. James, "God's sillie vassall," had the will but not the consistency to assert the prerogative in its extreme form. Charles had the obstinacy to assert it, but, happily for England, not the strength to maintain it. Profoundly convinced that God had appointed him to govern England, he regarded the nation as subjects whose only duty was to obey their sovereign and pay the taxes, and Parliament as the instrument by which the nation could express its obedience and support his personal government. When Parliament declined to adopt this simple idea of its duties, the king dismissed it, and for eleven years (1629-1640) governed without so turbulent and inconvenient a council.

Further, the Stuart theory was "no bishop, no king." Accordingly the Episcopal Church was favoured with the royal support on the distinct understanding that it should maintain the king's prerogative, preach the doctrine of passive obedience, and lend the sanction of religion to the arbitrary power of the throne. This the bishops, and more particularly Laud, backed by the universities, and by a considerable section of the clergy, very readily did. The king might coerce his subjects politically, with the support of the Church, through the arbitrary court of the Star Chamber, and in return the Church, through the Court of High Commission, might with the king's assistance force all Englishmen into the religious system approved by the bishops.

There is no reason to think that the king was conscious of doing anything illegal; on the contrary, he believed that he was justified by law and by the divine will. Nor is there any reason to think that the bishops were conscious of betraying their country or religion; "little Doctor Laud" was as sincere a man in his way as Oliver Cromwell was in his. But here was the plain fact: if Charles I. and Archbishop Laud had succeeded, the liberties of England would have perished, and the England of to-day would have been in the condition of Spain or Russia. Instead

of being the leader of the world in political
progress and representative institutions, England
would have been herself arrested, and her parliamentary history would have become a memory of
past and happier centuries instead of a hope for
ages to come.

The task to be accomplished, then, was to
shatter the system represented by the king and
Archbishop Laud.   And what a task it was, we
who only see it accomplished once and for ever
can hardly conceive.   England was, as she is,
passionately attached to the monarchical idea.
The splendid and pathetic devotion of Strafford,
Bristol, Hyde, Montrose—their name was legion
in those stormy years—to the person of Charles,
who had no great gift of arousing enthusiasm or
devotion to himself, is the best witness of the
obstacles which had to be overcome.   The future
of England was being jeopardised ; her liberties
were being quietly filched away, and she, broadly
speaking, loved to have it so.   The guardians of
her welfare along constitutional paths were not
sufficiently powerful to resist the throne.   Sir
John Eliot, the noblest soul that England had
found to utter her voice, she allowed, at the king's
bidding, to be thrown into the Tower, and there

to languish and die.   The great Pym was able
to impeach Strafford and bring him to the
block; but to impeach the chief cause of the
mischief was not within his power.   Nor could
any parliamentary leader, it appears, have restored
the country to her liberties.   "The chief cause of
the mischief"—yes, Charles himself, by his peculiar
virtues and vices, was the *fons et origo malorum*.
Sincere and religious, yet shifty and untrustworthy; counting it a divine obligation to
maintain his regal rights, but feeling no moral
obligation to maintain them by straightforward
dealing; gifted with a determination which
showed itself more frequently in obstinacy than
in courage; sufficiently bad as a king to justify
extreme measures, sufficiently good as a man to
make any attack on him wear the appearance of
sacrilege;—the king was the great difficulty.   If
the task was to be done, and if England was to
be saved, there must be a man who could not
only assail an ancient throne which had violated
the rights of the people and made religion itself
an instrument of tyranny, but could also deal with
the well-meaning, perverse, and slippery man who
at the time occupied the throne.

No one could have foreseen at the outset that

the dethronement of the king would be necessary to the discharge of the task. No one could have dreamed that a more fatal possibility still might arise. But as Charles was what he was, the man to deal with him must be one prepared for all extremities. At first it did not seem essential, in order to secure religious liberty, that Episcopacy, and even Presbyterianism, should go by the board; but so inveterate was the habit of spiritual tyranny that a church system was dangerous in proportion as it was strong. And if religion, and not simply irreligion, was to break the neck of spiritual tyranny, there must be one in whom religion was strong enough to shatter the strongest churches. Certainly for this stupendous task a remarkable man was needed; and such a man was prepared, a kinsman, by a collateral branch, of that Thomas Cromwell, Earl of Essex, who had been in Henry VIII.'s time dubbed *malleus monachorum;* another Cromwell was to be the *mallet* to break kings and prelates, and to pave the way for the freedom of his country and of religion.

"I was by birth a gentleman," said Oliver in one of his speeches,[1] "living neither in any considerable height nor yet in obscurity." His family

---

[1] Carlyle, Speech iii. vol. iv. 47. (The references to

was one that had been enriched by the suppression of the monasteries.   Hinchinbrook, which still stands, fair and stately, at the entrance into his native town, Huntingdon, was the seat of his great-uncle, Sir Henry Cromwell, a profuse and hospitable man, known as *The Golden Knight*. His uncle, Sir Oliver, welcomed and royally entertained his sovereign, James I., when Oliver was four years old.   His father, Robert Cromwell, though a second son, had a fair patrimony and married a Steward, who brought him further property in Ely.   When, therefore, the father died in 1617, Oliver, a boy of eighteen—he was born 25th April 1599—was well provided for, and when his maternal grandfather, Sir Thomas Steward, died in 1636 he became tolerably wealthy. His schooling was given him by Dr. Thomas Beard at Huntingdon Grammar School, a fervent Puritan divine, to whom a grateful pupil referred in the first public speech of his which has come down to us.   It is more than likely " that to Dr. Beard Oliver owed his conversion." [1]

For a year, from April 22, 1616, the boy was

Carlyle's *Letters and Speeches* are to the five volume edition of 1873, published by Chapman and Hall.)

[1] Gardiner, *Civil War*, vii. 54.

a fellow-commoner at Sydney Sussex College,
Cambridge, but his father's death brought him from
the university to manage his property.   He found
time, however, to pay a visit to London, with the
view of completing his education by the study
of law.   And there he took to himself a wife,
Elizabeth, the daughter of Sir James Bourchier.
They were married in St. Giles's, Cripplegate, on
August 22, 1620.   It was thirty years after that
he wrote to her from the field of Dunbar a letter
which tells us much of him and something of
her :—

"My dearest, I have not leisure to write much,
but I could chide thee that in many of thy letters
thou writest to me that I should not be unmindful
of thee and of thy little ones.   Truly if I love thee
not too well I think I err not on the other hand
much. Thou art dearer to me than any other
creature; let that suffice." [1]   And she in reply
—"My dearest, I wonder you should blame me for
writing no oftener, when I have sent thee three to
one. . . . Truly my life is but half a life in your
absence, did not the Lord make it up in Himself,
which I must acknowledge to the praise of His
grace." [2]

[1] Carl., Letter cxliii., vol. iii. 51.   [2] Carl. iii. 105.

If they were lovers in 1620 it is clear that they
were still lovers at the end.   In 1626 his third
son, Richard,[1] afterwards the Protector, was born,
on which occasion he wrote to his Cambridge
friend, Downhall : "Loving Sir, make me so
much your servant as to be godfather unto my
child." [2]   The tender husband was also the
tenderest of fathers.   All through the tumultuous
life runs the steady current of paternal solicitude,
reciprocated love, and, in times of bereavement,
of incurable grief.   It was a daughter's death that
hastened his own.

Oliver returned to Huntingdon, and was soon
immersed in business as a country gentleman.
But his soul was deeply exercised.   The sense of
sin was upon him.   Like Bunyan, like all the

---

[1] Carl. v. 148.   It was the death of his eldest son
Robert, in 1639, which gave him the "dagger at his
heart" mentioned in the closing days.   The list of his
children is :—

    1. Robert, who died at the age of eighteen.
    2. Oliver, killed in the Civil War, 1644.
    3. Richard, the Protector.
    4. Henry, the capable Deputy of Ireland.
    5. Bridget, married to Ireton and then to Fleetwood.
    6. Elizabeth, married to John Claypole.
    7. Mary, married to Lord Fauconberg.
    8. Frances, married to Robert Rich.

[2] Carl. v. 157.

1629 Church's greatest sons, he had to go through the Slough of Despond before he reached the wicket gate and the Cross. Looking back on that period long afterwards he wrote : " I lived in and loved darkness, and hated light. I was chief, the chief of sinners. This is true, I hated godliness, yet God had mercy on me." Carlyle, on the strength of Warwick's *Memoirs*, attributes this spiritual struggle to a splenetic and hypochondriac disposition, and utters the beautiful comment, " Our sorrow is the inverted image of our nobleness. The depth of our despair measures what capability and height of claim we have to hope." [1] But this was not a movement of the spleen; it was the awaking of the soul. " Who ever tasted that the Lord is gracious without some sense of self, vanity, and badness ? " Cromwell afterwards wrote to his daughters. And when after a long struggle he found Christ, and sealed that covenant with Him which was the turning-point of his life, and the constant theme of his letters and conversation, the melancholy passed away for ever.

The consideration in which he was held at Huntingdon is proved by the fact that in the

[1] Carl. vol. i. 43.

Parliament of 1628,[1] the great Parliament which Aet. 30 drew up the Petition of Right, Oliver, though only twenty-nine, was returned as member for his native town. It was on February 11, 1629, that he made his first speech in that House with which his future work was to be intimately entwined. It was—how characteristic it seems— a protest against "one, Dr. Alablaster, who did at the Spital preach in a sermon tenets of Popery," and Dr. Neile, bishop of Winchester, had abetted him in it, and had reprimanded Dr. Beard, our old schoolmaster, for refuting it! There was the Oliver who was to shake England and Rome. On March 10 this third Parliament of Charles I. was abruptly dissolved.

In the summer of 1630 a new Charter was granted to Huntingdon, and Oliver, seeing that it placed the property of the borough at the disposal of the aldermen, spoke, as he afterwards admitted,

[1] He appears at Westminster March 17, 1627, as it was dated then, when New Year's Day was still on March 25. But to avoid confusion, I follow Professor Gardiner in always translating the dates between 1st January and 25th March into our modern usage. Carlyle kept Oliver's own dating, with the result that much pains is required to remember exactly where we are.

1630 " in heat and passion " against the Mayor. He
was summoned to London and had to appear
before the Council. The matter was referred to
the Earl of Manchester as arbitrator, who sustained
his objections.   But this seems to have determined him to leave Huntingdon.   For early next
year he moved to St. Ives, where he lived, quietly
managing a grazing farm and interesting himself
in local affairs, until 1636.   During these years
the agitation in the country was rising.   It was in
1637 that John Hampden, who was Oliver's first
cousin, refused to admit the demand for ship-money
made by the arbitrary writ of the king.   But the
first letter of Oliver, which belongs to this period,
dated January 11, 1636, shows no sign that he was
even observing public events,—London citizens
mutilated, branded, pilloried, for refusing the
illegal exaction, and Scotland risen in a flame
against Dr. Laud's enforced Episcopacy.   It is
simply a note of gratitude to a worthy London
citizen who had established a lectureship in the
county of Huntingdon, " in the which," he says,
" you placed Dr. Wells, a man of goodness and
industry and ability to do good every way; not
short of any I know in England; and I am persuaded that sithence his coming, the Lord hath by

him wrought much good among us."[1]   Soon after,
the family moved to Ely (1636), and there Oliver
found himself espousing the cause of the Commoners who were suffering in the Earl of Bedford's
scheme for draining the Fens.   It would seem
that he did not oppose the king in council, as
Carlyle thought, but rather sided with the king
against Bedford, a creditable attitude to take, as
Bedford was a friend, and Oliver's cousin, St.
John, was Bedford's counsel.   In this simple act
of mercy and justice the country squire was engaged while England was taking fire.   And the
Second Letter of Carlyle's collection, dated October 13, 1638, and addressed to his cousin, Mrs.
St. John, is an ebullition of simple personal piety:
" If here I may honour my God either by doing or
suffering, I shall be most glad.   Truly, no poor
creature hath more cause to put himself forth in
the cause of his God than I.   I have had plentiful
wages beforehand, and I am sure I shall never
earn the least mite."[2]

That was the keynote of his life.   He was
doing the work nearest at hand, with no expectation of being drawn into the stormy arena of public
affairs.   But his whole soul was possessed with

---

[1] Carl. i. 77.   [2] *Ibid.* 87.

1640 the sense of what he owed to Christ who had saved him. Whatever he would do he would do for Christ's sake. And as all was a debt before-hand, he would neither seek nor expect any reward. " Pray for me that he who hath begun a good work would perfect it in the day of Christ."

But the imperative call was coming. In April 1640, the distressed king, in spite of his victory over Hampden, was compelled to summon a parliament in order to raise money to carry on his war with refractory Scotland. Oliver was returned as member for Cambridge. The " Short Parlia-ment" was dismissed in three weeks.

But on November 3 the famous Long Parlia-ment assembled, and Oliver was again member for Cambridge. Happily a graphic description of him in those early days has been preserved in Warwick's *Memoirs*. Warwick, also a member of this Parliament, saw him one day on his feet in the House. " Very ordinarily apparelled," says the courtly writer, " for it was a plain cloth suit, which seemed to have been made by an ill country tailor; his linen was plain and not very clean; and I remember a speck or two of blood upon his linen band which was not much larger than his collar. His hat was without a hat-band. His

stature was of a good size; his sword stuck close
to his side; his countenance swoln and reddish,
his voice sharp and untunable, and his eloquence
full of fervour. For the subject matter would
not bear much of reason, it being on behalf of a
servant of Mr. Trynne's, who had dispersed libels
against the queen for her dancing and such-like
innocent and courtly sports. I sincerely profess
it lessened much my reverence unto that
great council, for this gentleman was very much
hearkened unto." [1]

A shabby, vehement, godly man, this was he
who had the great task to do. With that sword
which stuck close to his side, and that untunable
voice, and that fiery heart of faith and purity and
love, he had to attempt the most difficult work
ever set before an Englishman.

On December 30 Cromwell brought in a Bill
for Annual Parliaments. No one in that House
was so able to appreciate the immediate practical
necessities of the situation. No one was less
influenced by theories or by far-off possibilities.
The reassembled Parliament must first secure that
it should not be suspended again, leaving the
king and Strafford and Laud unchecked to work

[1] Warwick's *Memoirs*, p. 247.

their will in England. In February 1641 we find him speaking vehemently against Laud and the other bishops. On March 1, Laud was lodged in the Tower. As Bishop Jeremy Taylor recognised, "The interest of the bishops is conjunct with the prosperity of the king. For they who have their livelihood from the king . . . are more likely to pay a tribute of exacter duty." It must always be remembered that the attack on Episcopacy was not an attack on a church system, but on a body of men who had made themselves the subservient tools of tyranny, just as the unanimous opposition to Rome was England's instinct of self-defence against the Papal claims which would destroy her liberty. It was this consideration that led Cromwell to unite with the Root-and-Branch policy for the extinction of Episcopacy.

In November came the Irish Rebellion and the horrible massacre of Protestants, which filled that generation of Englishmen with a pitiless resentment, and kindled the fires in Cromwell's breast destined, ten years later, to burn in ruthless vengeance at Drogheda and Wexford. In that same month came the Great Remonstrance, which was supported by Cromwell with triumphant confidence. It was carried on November 22,

and as the members left the House Falkland and Aet. 43
Cromwell met, the most pathetic and the most
forcible figures of a tumultuous period. It was
to Falkland that Cromwell said, "If the Remonstrance had been rejected, I would have
sold all I had the next morning and never
have seen England any more; and I know
there are many other honest men of this same
resolution."[1]

On January 4, 1642, came the arrest of the
five members. On the 12th Charles left Whitehall, not to return till he should come to die on
the scaffold after seven terrible years. He had
brought things to this pass, that war alone could
settle the account between him and his Parliament.
How Oliver regarded the matter may be judged
by two letters dated in March and April of this
year. "It is not improbable that the king may
go through Huntingdon on his way to Stamford.
Pray keep all steady and let no peace be broken.
Beg of all to be silent, or it may mar our peace-
able settling of this sad business. . . . The Lord has
hardened the king's heart more and more; he has
refused to hear reason, or to care for our cause, or
religion or peace. Let our friends have notice of

[1] Gardiner, *History*, x. 78.

1642 our sad news."[1]   " He is more shifty every day,"
Oliver wrote in May. With a man so obstinately
confident of his own prerogative and so incapable
of plain dealing, arguments and verbal appeals
were thrown away. His word could not be
trusted. The sword must be drawn. But Cromwell for one was not in doubt about the issue.
" I do feel myself lifted on by a strange force, I
cannot tell why. By night and by day I am urged
forward on the great work. . . . Therefore shall I
not fear what man can do unto me. I feel He
giveth me the light to see the great darkness that
surrounds us at noonday. . . . I seek daily and do
nothing without first so seeking the Lord."[2]   This
was written in July. On August 15 Cromwell
seized the Castle of Cambridge and captured the
plate, valued at £20,000, which the loyal university
was despatching to the king, and on the 22nd,
the Civil War began by Charles rearing his standard at Nottingham. When a king is at war with
the constitutional representatives of his people,
his victory portends the ruin of the constitution ;
their victory, the ruin of the king. On that
August day 1642 all the signs pointed to the

[1] *Squire Papers*, see Carl. ii. 270.
[2] Carl. p. 273.

victory of the king. Round him at once rallied Aet. 43
all the gentry, all who were trained in arms, and
on his side were all the traditional sentiments of a
conservative people. That those signs were falsi-
fied, and that the Constitution triumphed, was
due essentially to one man, and that was the man
who had been, all unknown to himself, silently
prepared for the great task.

CHAPTER II

" The man Cromwell is a wise and active head, universally
well-beloved, as religious and stout."

1642 WHEN the war broke out Cromwell was well on
in his forty-third year, nor had he ever had any
experience of military affairs. But he, like his
cousin John Hampden, and several other members
of Parliament, offered his services in the field.
The Earl of Essex had been, so long before as November 6, 1641, on Cromwell's motion, appointed
to command the train bands south of the Trent
on behalf of the Parliament; the Earl of Bedford
was general of the horse; and the member for Cambridge was at once made captain of his 67th troop.
He took with him his eldest surviving son, Oliver,
who was barely twenty years of age, and this was
the first sacrifice he had to make in the war. The

young Oliver was appointed to a cornetcy in the Aet. 43
8th troop, and was killed just before Marston
Moor. How the father suffered in such a loss we
learn from that cry on his deathbed in reference
to the death of his first-born. "It went to my
heart like a dagger, indeed it did."

Carlyle tells us, on Heath's authority, that
Cromwell learned the mechanical art of soldiering
from Dulbier, a man of Dutch birth, who afterwards changed sides and was killed at St. Neot's
by Fairfax's troops.[1] This is quite conceivable;
but what made Oliver one of the greatest soldiers
in the world was not a knowledge of "the
mechanical art of soldiering" at all. It would be
nearer the truth to say, that he learnt to make
armies and to win battles in his Bible and on his
knees. His personal fearlessness arose from an
absolute confidence in his cause, and in his God.
And the quickness of sight and judgment which
enabled him to seize the essential point in a strate-
gical position and gained him most of his victories
was of the nature of inspiration. Every letter he
wrote from a battlefield unquestioningly attributes
the action and the result to God. Never does
there escape from his pen a hint that he had any-

[1] Gardiner, *Civil War*, iv. 161.

1642 thing to do with it. Self-complacency was out of the question. "It is the Lord's doing and it is marvellous in our eyes," that is the tone of all his despatches. Quite naturally this has been interpreted as hypocrisy. But the result of this interpretation is that Cromwell becomes an enigma, and the lesson of his life is lost.

As this was the source of his own military capacity, it is not surprising that he introduced a new method of enlisting soldiers. For the first three years of the war the Parliamentary Army was composed of local levies, raised and maintained by county associations. Of these the Eastern Association, in which Oliver was the life and soul, was far the most efficient. The reason of this was given in a speech of his own to the Parliament of 1657. "At my first going out into this engagement I saw our troops were beaten on every hand." That was true. In the first campaign, and up to Marston Moor, the Royal troops very generally had the advantage. "I had a very worthy friend then, Mr. John Hampden. 'Your troops,' said I, 'are most of them old decayed serving men and tapsters and such kind of fellows, and their troops are gentlemen's sons; do you think that the spirits of such base and mean

fellows will ever be able to encounter gentlemen Aet. 43
that have honour and courage and resolution in
them? You must have men of a spirit that will go
on as far as gentlemen will go.' He did think
that I talked a good notion, but an impracticable
one. Truly I told him that I could *do* somewhat
in it."[1] He *did* somewhat in it. He formed
troops of devout Christian men, who fought for a
great cause in a great spirit. He did not ask for
gentlemen, but for men of a spirit that would go
as far as gentlemen or farther. They were men of
God. Woe betide them if they were not. "Hang
the fellow out of hand," was an order given on
15th March 1642, "and I am your warrant. For
he shot a boy at Pilton-bee by the Spinney, the
widow's son, her only support; so God and man
must rejoice at his punishment."[2] If soldiers of
his were found looting, or stealing, they were
promptly handed over to the enemy for punishment.[3] The name Ironside was given to Cromwell

---

[1] Carl. v. 12. [2] *Ibid.* ii. 276.

[3] "As for Col. Cromwell," says a news letter of May
1643, "he hath 2000 brave men well-disciplined; no
man swears but he pays his twelvepence; if he be drunk
he is set in the stocks, or worse; the countries where they
come leap for joy of them, and come in and join with
them. How happy were it if all the forces were thus
disciplined."

1643 himself by Prince Rupert after Marston Moor.   It
was at Pontefract, so late as 1648, that the name
was transferred to his men.[1]   But from the first
the men caught his own spirit.   Like him they
were invincible.   Where Cromwell and his troops
appeared victory came in the train.   Essex and
the Earl of Manchester and Walter were good
soldiers of the ordinary sort, and they were
beaten or frustrated by the Royalists.   Cromwell
and his troops were soldiers of quite an extraordinary sort.   A power not their own worked with
them.   It was the power of godliness.   They were
bound to come to the front, and they were bound
to win.

Cromwell was present in the first engagement
of the war at Edgehill, October 23, 1642, and his
troops stood firm in that ambiguous field.   But
his first victory was won near Grantham on
May 13, 1643.   The enemy waited to receive him.
" Our men charging fiercely upon them, by God's
providence they were immediately routed and all
ran away, and we had the execution of them two
or three miles." [2]   It was, however, at Gainsborough Fight on July 28, where young Charles
Cavendish was slain in arms, that the name

---

[1] Gardiner, *Civil War*, iv. 178.   [2] Carl. i. 129.

which was to ring through Europe was first Aet. 44 distinctly heard. In October, Cromwell, now lieutenant-general in Manchester's army, gained a battle at Winceby. His horse was killed at the first charge, and fell upon him; and as he rose up he was knocked down again by the gentleman who charged him, but afterwards recovered a poor horse in a soldier's hands and bravely mounted himself again. The enemy were chased, slaughtered, drowned, and dispersed. Grantham, Gainsborough, Winceby, were the opening of this soldier's career. On July 2, 1644, came the decisive battle of Marston Moor. "Is Cromwell there?" asked Rupert of a prisoner. "And will they fight? If they will, they shall have fighting enough." When the prisoner brought the message, Cromwell's answer was, "If it please God so shall he."[1]

The Scotch under the Earl of Leven fought side by side with the English Parliamentarians. But the right wing under the two Fairfaxes was overpowered by Goring's furious charge. Leven fled from the field. The position was entirely retrieved by Cromwell, who had kept his men well in hand, and by Crawford who commanded the Infantry of the Eastern Association. Cromwell

[1] Gard. *Civil War*, i. 376.

1644 chased Rupert to the gates of York, wheeled
round and routed the victorious Goring. The
king's army retreated, leaving 4000 slain on the
field. " Truly England and the Church of God
hath had a great favour from the Lord," wrote
the lieutenant-general, " in this great victory given
unto us, such as the like never was since this war
began. It had all the evidences of an absolute
victory obtained by the Lord's blessing upon the
godly party principally. We never charged but
we routed the enemy. The left which I commanded, being our own horse, saving a few Scots
in our rear, beat all the Prince's horse. God
made them as stubble to our swords." And then
he proceeds to comfort his correspondent whose
son had been slain in the fight, remembering his
loss of his own Oliver three months before. " You
may do all things by the strength of Christ. Seek
that and you shall easily bear your trial. Let this
public mercy to the Church of God make you to
forget your private sorrow." [1]

At Marston Moor Cromwell had shown that a
godly party could face and overcome the Royalist
chivalry. But meanwhile Essex and Waller in
the west had been beaten and had lost their

[1] Carl. i. 167.

armies; and on October 27, supplied by a con- Aet. 45
fiding Parliament with new forces, and supported
by Manchester and Cromwell, they met the king
at Newbury,—it was the second battle that had
taken place near that town,—and neglected to
improve their advantage. The truth was that
Manchester did not wish to beat the king. He
hoped for concessions and a reconciliation. Cromwell alone grasped the situation and dared to
recognise that until the king was beaten there
could be no peace. Phlegmatic and timid noble-
men like Essex and Manchester were horrified by
the lieutenant-general's reputed saying, that "If
he met the king in battle he would fire his pistol
at the king as at another."

There must be a change. On November 25
Cromwell from his place in the House of Commons
charged Manchester with lukewarmness; and in
December he advocated the formation of the New
Model, an army which should be raised and supported not by local associations but by Parliament,
and to which men should be admitted without
signing the Covenant. He had from the first
been reluctant to take the Covenant himself, and
his contact with the Scots had filled him with
mistrust of them and of their intolerant Presby-

1645 terianism. The Scots on the other hand began to speak of him as "that darling of the Sectaries." His notion of religion as a direct action of the spirit of God upon the spirit of man, which was the essence of Independency, made him always more afraid of quenching the spirit than of facing the anarchy which is always liable to attend a complete liberty of prophesying.

The New Model was finally accepted in April 1645. A Self-denying Ordinance, debarring all members of Parliament from command in the army, designed to get rid of Essex, Manchester, and Denbigh, and of course excluding Cromwell himself, was carried by the Commons, but rejected by the Lords. It was evidently Cromwell's intention to retire from the military service, which was at best a painful burden to him, and to discharge his mission in Parliament and in the Committee of both kingdoms, of which he had been made a member in February 1643. It must always be borne in mind that he was a soldier only by accident. But the Parliamentary Army was seething with discontent, ill-found and ill-paid; while the news-writers of the day pointed out that Cromwell's men were conspicuous by their readiness at all times "to obey any ordinance of

Parliament, and that there was none of them Aet. 46
known to do the least wrong by plunder or any
abuse to any country people where they came."[1]
Angry Presbyterians were threatening to impeach
him in the House, but in the army he had made
his ineffaceable mark. In spite of Self-denying
Ordinances this lieutenant-general could not be
spared. Sir Thomas Fairfax was in supreme
command. But Cromwell was hastily despatched
to meet Rupert near Oxford, and by his rapid and
effective movements made it evident to Fairfax
that he must be lieutenant-general still. Parliament yielded to the request.[2] Meanwhile in the
negotiations known as the Treaty of Uxbridge
Charles, "more shifty than ever," had been demonstrating the impossibility of coming to any
secure terms with him. One day he had proposed
to the Commissioners of the Parliament that both
armies should be disbanded and he would return
in person to Westminster. The day before he
had written to his wife—and this was one of the
fatal letters found in his cabinet after the battle
of Naseby—"As for trusting the rebels, either

[1] Gard. *Civil War*, ii. 178.
[2] *Ibid.* ii. 238. The appointment passed the Commons
four days before the battle of Naseby.

1645 by going to London or disbanding my army before a peace, do no ways fear my hazarding so cheaply or foolishly; for I esteem the interest thou hast in me at a far dearer rate, and pretend to have a little more wit—at least by the sympathy that is betwixt us—than to put myself in the reverence of perfidious rebels." [1]

With such a man, though an anointed king and the defender of the Church, there could be no peace until he was broken. But Glamorgan in Ireland and Montrose in Scotland were successfully maintaining the Royal cause; and unless Fairfax was more determined than Essex, and the New Model more efficient than the old levies, notwithstanding Marston Moor, the king had every prospect of winning the day. He despised the New Model. On May 31 he stormed Leicester. On June 10 he was at Daventry, determined to attack the Eastern Association. But Cromwell appeared in the army of Fairfax with a promise of 4000 horse and 1000 foot from his redoubtable Fens, and the Royal Army was so perturbed by the news that it decided to avoid an engagement. It moved northwards, but Fairfax pursued. Harrison, eager to smite the enemies of the Lord,

---

[1] Gard. *Civil War*, ii. 129.

was sent to reconnoitre around Daventry, while Ireton went forward to outmarch the enemy. It was impossible to escape. Charles had 7500, Fairfax 13,600. On June 14 the armies faced one another a mile or so on the north road from Naseby. It was Cromwell's eye which saw where the army could be most advantageously placed. It was Cromwell's heart that glowed with the confidence of victory. " I can say this," he wrote afterwards, " that when I saw the enemy draw up and march in gallant order towards us, and we a company of poor ignorant men to seek how to order our battle, the general having commanded me to order all the horse, I could not—riding alone about my business—but smile out to God in praises in assurance of victory, because God would, by things that are not, bring to naught things that are, of which I had great assurance—and God did it." [1]

Yes, God did it, but Cromwell was his instrument. For again, as at Marston Moor, it was the terrific charge of Cromwell's horse which changed the balance of the day, when the Parliamentary left had been broken by Rupert and the Cavaliers. It was Cromwell who re-formed the line, and met

[1] Gard. *Civil War*, ii. 247.

1645 the temporary victors with a quiet and unbroken front. The great soldier never lost his presence of mind, never blundered for a moment. How could he, held in such a hand? The Royalists were routed, and the king would never again lift up his head. The battle had lasted from 10 to 1 P.M. That same night from Harborough Cromwell sent his despatch to Lenthall, Speaker of the House:

"Sir, this is none other than the hand of God; and to Him alone belongs the glory, wherein none are to share with Him. Honest men served you faithfully in this action"—yes, these were the Independents, scorned as "sectaries," who formed a large part of the New Model, and who come now under the peculiar protection and favour of Cromwell. "Sir, they are trusty; I beseech you in the name of God not to discourage them. He that ventures his life for the liberty of his country, I wish he trust God for the liberty of his conscience and you for the liberty he fights for."

Naseby was practically the end of the First Civil War; but this last sentence reveals a danger which was to lead to divisions between the conquerors and to another internecine war. The king was overthrown, but intolerance also had to die, and the principle of spiritual liberty had to be vindicated, if Cromwell's task was to be done.

Before we pass to the developments which tore asunder the victors of Naseby, we may follow Cromwell westward in his successful work of stamping out the embers of the war. On July 10 Cromwell from the height near Long Sutton watched with devout thankfulness one of the bravest feats ever performed. Major Bethel, a type of these military saints, and Desborough, with a handful of men, flew at Goring's army, which was three times their number, and annihilated it. Writing from Langport, the scene of the battle, he says: "Thus you have Long Sutton mercy added to Naseby mercy. And to see this, is it not to see the face of God?"

Those words carry us to the heart of Oliver's conviction. He hoped, as he once said, that he did not make too much of dispensations, but in these decisive events he saw the work of God proceeding before his eyes.[1] In absolute faith he drew the sword; in absolute faith he accepted the issue as the decision of God. The results of these

[1] Between April 1645 and August 1646 the New Model was successful in sixty encounters, took 50 strong places, 1000 cannon, 40,000 arms, and 250 colours.

1645 battles were to him as clearly the revelation of
God as any words of Scripture. And this must
be remembered if we are to rightly judge his
unswerving purpose to secure the fruits of the
victory. On August 4 he routed the clubmen
on Hambledon Hill, near Shaftesbury, after vainly
trying to induce the deluded peasants to lay
down their extemporised arms. On September
11 Bristol was stormed. His account of the
storming in a letter to Lenthall is a notable
despatch. " All this is none other than the work
of God. He must be a very atheist that doth not
acknowledge it." And then he passes on to say—
though the House foolishly omitted this part of
the document—how Presbyterians and Independents had fought in the same spirit of faith and
prayer, how they had "the same presence and
answer, they agree here and have no means of
difference, pity it is it should be otherwise any-
where." [1]   Prince Rupert rode out of Bristol amid
the execrations of the people, and begged from
Fairfax a thousand muskets to protect his escort
to Oxford, a request which was generously granted.
In this first civil war a spirit of chivalry prevailed,
which was painfully wanting in the outbreak of

[1] Gard. *Civil War*, ii. 320.

1648, when Englishmen confronting Royalist Aet. 46
armies, felt that they were dealing with Scotch
and Irish invaders who had been for centuries
their hereditary foes.

On September 23 the strong castle of Devizes
surrendered to Cromwell. On October 5 he
took Winchester, and wrote to the Speaker—
"God is not weary of doing you good." On the
14th he stormed Basing House, which had held
out for four years, the seat of the Catholic
Marquis of Winchester. Oliver, says Hugh
Peters, the chaplain, had " spent much time with
God in prayer the night before." As the
defenders had refused the summons they were put
to the sword. " I thank God," he wrote to the
Commons, " I can give you a good account of
Basing. God exceedingly abounds in His goodness to us, and will not be weary until righteousness and peace meet together, and until He hath
brought forth a glorious work for the happiness
of this poor kingdom." [1]

On January 8, 1646, Cromwell surprised Lord
Wentworth's Brigade at Bovey Tracey, and by the
end of the month all Devonshire, plundered and
abused as it had been by Goring and the Royalists,

[1] Carl. i. 211.

1646 was eager to enlist in Fairfax's army. "We are come," said Cromwell to them, "to set you if possible at liberty from your taskmasters." The war came to an end with Astley's defeat at Stow-on-the-Wold, March 21. "You have done your work," said the brave veteran, "and may go play, unless you will fall out amongst yourselves." [1] The war for the time was over, and the king had now no hope but in the Scots, and in the divisions of his enemies. Cromwell could write with a thankful heart, "Thanks be given to God, I trust now all will be well for this nation, and an enduring peace be, to God His glory and our prosperity." He was always eager to sheathe the sword, and it was a stern necessity which drove him to draw it three times more before the enduring peace could be established.

---

[1] Gard. *Civil War*, iii. 80.

CHAPTER III

TO THE END OF THE SECOND CIVIL WAR

1646–1647

"To see this, is it not to see the face of God?"—(Carlyle, v. 182).

PARLIAMENT was victorious, and the instrument **1646** of its victory had been—no one could deny it— the religious conviction of the Independents embodied in their great captain, Cromwell himself. But Parliament in the main was Presbyterian. Since the fall of Episcopacy, the Covenant had been the foundation, and Presbyterianism the form, of the English Church. In principle, and still more in practice, the Presbyterians were no less opposed to the Sectaries than the Royalists themselves. Their sentiment is reflected in Richard Baxter, who visited the army after Naseby, and obtained a chaplaincy in Whalley's regiment. He was scandalised to find that Crom-

1646 well believed in liberty of conscience, and in leaving every man not only to hold, but to preach, what views he pleased. Equally scandalised was he to find that in the army the king was regarded as a tyrant and an enemy, with whom it was impossible to come to terms; and the nobility were treated as not indispensable. In a word, concluded the good man, "They thought God's providence would cast the trust of religion and the kingdom upon them as conquerors . . . *per fas aut nefas*, by law or without it, they were resolved to take down, not only bishops, and liturgy and ceremonies," for which, worthy soul, he was quite prepared, "but all that did withstand their way. They most honoured the Separatists, Anabaptists, and Antinomians; but Cromwell and his council took on themselves to join themselves to no party, but to be for the liberty of all."

Indeed in the army there were men like Ireton, and out of it there were impassioned doctrinaires, like John Lilburne, who had conceived that Democratic form of government, which only now after two centuries and a half is becoming possible.[1] They were bent on establish-

---

[1] The programme of the army was Republicanism, sovereignty of Parliament, annual or biennial elections,

ing it out of hand, and of using a victorious army Aet. 47
to effect the establishment. Cromwell had warm
sympathy with their ideals, but he was no doctrinaire, and he knew that they were attempting the
impossible. For the better part of a year, from
June 1646 to June 1647 he strove in the face
of obloquy and humiliation to keep the peace
between the two opposing parties. He could, as
we have seen, well bear with both if only they
would bear with one another. He took his stand
on the authority of Parliament. He maintained
the right of Parliament to control the army.
He pleaded with the Presbyterians not to suppress
the sectaries, and with the sectaries to find their
due place within the borders of a Presbyterian
establishment. Only when the blundering and
intolerance of the Presbyterians in Parliament had
frustrated this noble purpose, did he, the practical
man to whom theories were of little value, identify
himself with the claims of the army, and in that
way incur the charge of being a turn-coat and a
hypocrite. The charge was unfounded, as a slight
attention to the course of events reveals.

local self-government, codification of the law, complete
religious liberty, and equal political rights. — Frederic
Harrison's *Life*, p. 114.

1646   In the spring of 1646 there was a double marriage in Oliver's house. His eldest daughter, Bridget, became the wife of Ireton, the great Independent, a man of deep but tolerant religious earnestness, commissary-general to Sir Thomas Fairfax. Bridget was twenty-two; her sister Elizabeth, only seventeen, at the same time became the wife of Claypole. This is how the affectionate father wrote to one, and of the other; it is dated from London, doubtless Drury Lane, where the Cromwells had taken up their residence: —" 25th October 1646. For my beloved daughter, Bridget Ireton. Dear daughter—I write not to thy husband, partly to avoid trouble, for one line of mine begets many of his, which I doubt makes him sit up too late. . . . Your sister Claypole is, I trust in mercy, exercised with some perplexed thoughts. . . . She seeks after what will satisfy. . . . Dear heart, press on; let not husband, let not anything cool thy affections after Christ. . . . That which is best worthy of love in thy husband is that of the image of Christ he bears. Look on that and love it best and all the rest for that." [1]

It is a happy chance that many of these letters from the inner circle of the family have survived

[1] Carl. i. 230.

among the letters which are burdened with the Aet. 47
great affairs of State. There is the same tender
love in all, the same constant solicitude for the
spiritual welfare of his children, and a further
proof, if further were needed, that in the domestic
virtues he came no whit behind the king whom it
was his stern duty to oppose.

The king had in April stolen away to the
Scotch army at Newark, and in June had ordered
Oxford to surrender. On February 16, 1647, he
moved to Holmby, and entered upon a series of
characteristic negotiations. He held out hopes
to the Presbyterians in Parliament that if he
were restored he would maintain them in their
position. His private letters and conversations
reveal that he had not the least intention of
fulfilling the promise. He had a deep attach-
ment to the Episcopal Church, so deep that
he was ready to prevaricate in order to restore
it. But the Presbyterians were hoodwinked.
They mistrusted the army, the backbone of
which consisted of Independents. They were
prepared to make terms with the king which
would leave every man in the army exposed to a
charge of treason. "There want not," wrote
Cromwell, "in all places men who have so much

1647 malice against the army as besots them." They were determined to disband it, with little or no regard for the vast arrears of pay. Cromwell, from his place in the House, watching the infatuated course which Denzill Holles and his supporters were taking, whispered one day to Edmund Ludlow, "These men will never leave till the army pull them out by the ears." The weakness of the Presbyterians was that they had no policy and no leader. In resisting the army their only hope was to replace the king, who was prepared to outwit them as soon as he regained power. "Charles was an ally who never failed to ruin any man or party that trusted in him."[1] The army was in a state of ferment; its agents—Agitators was the old name—were in treaty with the House, endeavouring to resist disbandment. Cromwell saw before him, what he dreaded more than anything else, military anarchy and domination. His deepest conviction was loyalty to Parliament, whose obedient servant he had always been; but now he learnt that the Presbyterian Parliament was negotiating for an invasion from Scotland, intending to seize the king at Holmby, and determined to undo at a stroke the work—the

[1] Gard. *Civil War*, iii. 274.

Lord's work—of four strenuous years. It was
under these circumstances that early in June
Cromwell slipped away from the House of
Commons and put himself at the head of those
who in the army were crying for "Justice!
Justice!" His only way of controlling the
army was to lead it, and to lead it involved
addressing a threat to London, and, as Parliament
had no intention of dissolving, a forcible dissolution of Parliament itself. This action of the
army was deplorable enough, though it was forced
upon it by the stupidity of the House; but it was
an indefinite advantage, if the action was to be
taken, that so wise and moderate a man as
Cromwell should be at its head. A letter
addressed to Cromwell nine years later probably
reveals what was actually the situation. "Sir
Gilbert Pickering," says the writer, "was pleased
in his garden privately to give me to understand
with how much unwillingness you were at last
drawn to head that violent and rash part of the
army at Triploe Heath, when they would not
disband. He did tell me you rode it out until
the third letter came to you from them, wherein
they peremptorily told you that if you would not
forthwith, nay presently, come and head them,

1647 they would go their own way without you. They
were resolved to do so, for they did see Presbytery,
London, and the Scots go in such ways as would
beget a new war and very fatal also." [1] Thus the
loyal servant of Parliament found himself forced
into an attitude of opposition to Parliament. In
the interest of the nation, and still more, as he
believed, in the interest of Christ, he was led to
resist a Parliament which had become an irrespon-
sible Oligarchy, and a restoration of the king
which would be fatal to Christian liberty.

But Cromwell's first effort was to come to
terms with the king. In July he insisted on
allowing Charles to enjoy the ministrations of his
Episcopal chaplain, which neither the Scots nor
the Presbyterian Parliament would for a moment
allow. He secured the king two days of happy
intercourse with his children at Caversham, and
afterwards told Berkeley, with tears flowing from
his eyes, the particulars of that affecting scene,
which he himself witnessed. "The king," he said,
"was the uprightest and most conscientious man
of his three kingdoms," though he wished the
king would be "more frank and not be tied so
strictly to narrow maxims." [2]

[1] Gard. *Civil War*, iii. 264.   [2] *Ibid*. iii. 319.

On August 6 the army entered London, Aet. 48
Fairfax—who was indisposed—in his carriage,
Cromwell on horseback at the head of his cavalry.
It was a momentous and perilous step. Cromwell
persuaded himself that it was not as an army, but
as Englishmen demanding their rights, that these
men were marched to the capital and stationed
around Westminster to coerce the impracticable
Holles, Stapleton, and their followers. " I know
nothing to the contrary," he said, " but that I am
as well able to govern the kingdom as either "
Holles or Stapleton.[1] It was the desperate
attempt which a strong man, forced to take
irregular means in a grave crisis, will often make
to represent his action to himself as regular. But
even if he had seen what it meant Cromwell
would still have acted without hesitation.

From September to the end of the year
Cromwell spared no effort in trying to come to
terms with the king, who was at Hampton Court,
until in November he escaped to Carisbrooke.
The *Heads of Proposals*, made by the army to
Charles, had fallen through. The violent spirits
in the army, known as the Levellers, were arriving
at the conclusion that nothing but deposition

[1] Gard. *Civil War*, iii. 351.

F

1647 from the throne afforded any basis of a settlement, and these men regarded Cromwell with suspicion. On October 20 he appeared in the House urging the re-establishment of the throne without delay, giving the strongest assurances that neither he nor Fairfax had any hand in *The Case for the Army,* a manifesto drawn up by Lilburne. He asserted that his aim during the whole war had been to strengthen and not to destroy monarchy.[1]

Writing from the army quarters at Putney in November to his cousin, Colonel Whalley, he says, "There are rumours abroad of some intended attempt on his majesty's person. . . . If any such thing should be done it would be accounted a most horrid act."[2]

But in the long tussle with the Levellers, and in the perpetual disappointment of all attempts to come to an understanding with Charles, he gradually found himself standing on a principle which was fatal to the monarchy, as it had hitherto existed. "Though the council of the army was not wedded and glued to forms of government, it acknowledged that the foundation and the supremacy is in the people—radically in them— and to be set down by them in their representa-

[1] Gard. *Civil War,* iii. 379.   [2] Carl. i. 265.

tives." [1] That was the conviction of doctrinaires
like Ireton and Lilburne ; it was slowly taking
possession of the practical head which would be
able to give it effect. The Independents were
democratic in the modern sense of the word ; they
also clung to the idea of religious toleration.
Lilburne and Marten would have toleration un-
limited ; Cromwell would extend it only to
opinions which were not dangerous to the State.
But a great gulf opened between them and the
Presbyterians, who, however attracted towards
democracy, were scandalised at the idea of
toleration ; and as they drew back from Cromwell
and the Independents they drew nearer to the
Royalists, who were at least agreed with them on
this point, and already harboured thoughts which
pointed not to the Commonwealth but to the
Restoration.

It was in the month of November that Cromwell's solicitude to save the king received a
severe shock. He had a spy among the king's
retinue who sent him word that the doom of the
Independents was sealed in the king's council, and
this could be proved if the bearer of a letter to
the queen could be intercepted. The messenger

[1] Gard. iii. 386.

1647 was to be in Holborn at the Blue Boar Inn at 10 o'clock, on his way to Dover. The letter was sewn up in his saddle. What followed Cromwell may tell in his own words : " We were at Windsor when we received this letter, and immediately Ireton and I resolved to take one trusty fellow with us, and with trooper's habits to go to the inn in Holborn . . . we set our man at the gate . . . and called for cans of beer. The sentinel gave notice that the man with the saddle was coming in. Upon this we immediately arose, and as the man was leading out his horse saddled, came up to him with drawn swords and told him that we were to search all that went in and out there, but as he looked like an honest man we would only search his saddle and dismiss him. Upon this we ungirt his saddle and carried it into the stall where we had been drinking, and left the horseman with our sentinel. Then ripping up one of the skirts of the saddle, we there found the letter of which we had been informed. As soon as we had the letter we opened it, in which we found the king had acquainted the queen that he was now courted by both of the factions, the Scotch Presbyterians and the army, and which bid fairest for him should have him, but he thought he should

close with the Scots sooner than the others. Upon
this we took horse and went to Windsor, and
finding we were not likely to have any tolerable
terms from the king, we immediately from that
time forward resolved his ruin." [1]

The story is of the nature of hearsay, but it has
the colour of truth. So late as March 28, 1648,
we find Cromwell making desperate efforts to
bring the king to terms, and incurring the suspicion
of his friends for his pertinacity. "I know God
has been above all ill reports," he writes to
Norton, "and will in His own time vindicate me ;
I have no cause to complain. The Lord's will be
done. For news out of the North there is little,
only the malignant party is prevailing in the
Parliament of Scotland." [2] But the truth began
to be clear to him. The king was scheming with
the Scotch, with the Irish, and even with the
Dutch, to come to his aid and set him again on his
throne. It was rumoured that already Hamilton
was marching from Scotland with a great army.
Certainly London was in a state of agitation, and
a rising in the city was only repressed by a desperate
charge of cavalry. And now in South Wales
Poyer was sweeping over Pembrokeshire and

---

[1] Gard. *Civil War*, iv. 29.   [2] Carl. i. 278.

1648 rallying the excitable people to stand for the king.
At the end of April that which had been dreaded
for a year loomed terribly real before earnest men;
the king was stirring up a new civil war. Then
occurred an event which brings us to the very heart
of Independency, and lays bare the inner movements of Cromwell's mind. The notables of the
army with the Agitators met for a prolonged
prayer meeting at Windsor. Cromwell entreated
the army to humble itself and ask God where the
sin lay, which was bringing this new evil upon the
nation. It was all terribly earnest. On their
knees these bronzed and battered men with many
tears reached a grim conclusion. The king had
not, as in 1642, joined with his sympathisers, but
with men whose whole position he disapproved,
the Presbyterians, to move a new war. If they
were to be gladdened again by the consciousness
of the Lord's presence, they must abandon hope
of settlement with one so conscientious and yet
so untrustworthy as the king. "Presently we
we were led to a clear agreement" that it was
our duty to go out and fight against those potent
enemies, with a humble confidence in the name of
the Lord only; that it was our duty, if ever the
Lord brought us back again in peace, to call

Charles Stuart, that man of blood, to an account Aet. 49
for the blood he had shed and the mischief he had
done to his utmost against the Lord's cause and
people in these poor nations.[1] Cromwell only
partly sympathised with this extreme measure.
But now he was despatched into South Wales to
quell the rising there. Kent was in insurrection,
the fleet was in mutiny. In Essex Sir Charles
Lucas occupied Colchester and defied, until August
28, the whole army of Fairfax.[2] Oliver with
his accustomed concentration and coolness girt
himself for his part of the task. On May 8 he
was at Gloucester inviting his tried veterans to
adventure themselves again in the old cause. On
that very day Colonel Horton gained a brilliant
victory over Laugharne and the Royalists at St.
Fagan's. On May 11, when Cromwell reached
Chepstow, he was able to write that the rising was
suppressed. Only the three castles of Chepstow,
Tenby, and Pembroke held out for the king. The
two first surrendered before the month was over.
Pembroke caused him more trouble. His siege
train was wrecked at the mouth of the Severn.

[1] Allen's narrative. Gard. iv. 120.
[2] Since March Sir Thomas Fairfax had become Lord
Fairfax by the death of his father.

1648 " I pray God," he wrote to Fairfax on June 28,
"teach this nation what the mind of God may
be in all this and what our duty is. Surely it is
not that our God would have our necks under a
yoke of bondage." [1]   On July 4 he recovered his
batteries, and on the 11th Pembroke surrendered.
In his report to Lenthall he says of Poyer and his
abettors : "They have sinned against so much light,
and against so many evidences of divine providence
going along with and prospering a just cause, in
the management of which they themselves had a
share." It was to him incredible that any one,
even Charles himself, could fail to see the manifest
decision of God in the events of the first war.
To him the iniquity of those who took part in this
second war, especially of the Presbyterians, seemed
"double," and there enters into his spirit a
severity which he had not shown before.

[1] Gard. iv. 167.

CHAPTER IV

THE KING'S DOOM

1648–1649

To Englishmen of the seventeenth century the 1648 Scotch were foreigners and ancient foes, the Irish were barbarians and idolaters. Charles, when his English supporters had been utterly and finally routed, turned, not unnaturally perhaps, to his subjects in Ireland and Scotland. Ormond held out hopes of bringing over an Irish army to deliver him. The Duke of Hamilton actually led a Scotch army into England for the same purpose. It was this more than anything else that sealed the king's doom and brought him to the block. A shudder of horror ran through England at the thought of the Irish savages, who had recently slaughtered 80,000, some reports said 200,000, Protestants, being brought to the rescue of the Royalist cause.

1648 And if the indignation was not so great the
resolution was equally firm when, on July 8, 1648,
Hamilton crossed the border with 10,500 men
and occupied Carlisle.   Unhappy, chivalrous Duke,
who, as Mrs. Wilson said, "lost his head at
London; folk said it wasna a very gude ane, but
it was aye a sair loss to him, puir gentleman." [1]
He was engaged on a hopeless task, bringing an
army of raw recruits to face the veterans of the
Parliament who were backed with all the fiery
purpose of England, and led by Oliver Cromwell,
his heart hot with wrath against infatuated men
that could not read the plain providences of God.
John Lilburne, the fanatical democrat, was rather
maliciously liberated by the Lords in order to
embarrass Cromwell; but "honest John" was in
no mood to play the Presbyterian game, and
turned upon his liberators.   Nine ships of the
fleet, afterwards joined by two more, had gone
over to the Royalists, and were on the Norfolk
coast with the Prince of Wales on board.   They
even blockaded the Thames and interfered with
London   trade.   But   no   trifling   hindrances
affected the rapid sweep of Cromwell northwards
to support Lambert, whose handful of men was

[1] *Old Mortality*, ch. v.

insufficient to oppose Hamilton and had to fall Aet. 49
back. On August 1 Cromwell was at Leicester.
" Our brigade," wrote one of the army in the
Moderate, " came hither to - day. Our long
marches, and want of shoes and stockings gives
discouragement to our soldiers, having received no
pay these many months to buy them, nor can we
procure any unless we plunder, which was never
heard of by any under the Lieutenant-General's
conduct, nor will be, though they march barefoot,
which many have done since our advance from
Wales."

In the breasts of those shoeless men, who in a
town of shoes, and with arms in their hands,
would not plunder, beat the heart of England.
Wrath, justice, faith in God, were a better
equipment than money and clothes.

On August 8 the force was at Doncaster.
And on the 9th Henry Lilburne the governor of
Tynemouth Castle, went over to the Royalists.
Meanwhile, Hamilton had reached Kendal. He
was joined by Monro with veterans from Ireland.
And now it was determined to march through
Lancashire. On the 13th Cromwell with 8600
men, after joining forces with Lambert, marched
from Knaresborough. Hamilton's army had swollen

1648 to more than 20,000, but Cromwell was in no mood to wait for further reinforcements. His heart was hot with indignation to hear that the Scots were stripping the cottages as they passed along, seizing the children as hostages for ransom, butchering the parents if they refused to pay. His one thought was to throw himself across the southward march of these invaders and robbers. On the 17th Hamilton arrived at Preston. Before the army could cross the Ribble Cromwell was upon them. The main body of the Scots were all in confusion. But Langdale, with 3600 Englishmen, faced the veterans of Cromwell about a mile on the north-eastern road from Preston. They fought like heroes, but after four hours' struggle they were beaten back upon the town. In the night the duke drew off his army to Wigan. Cromwell gave chase in the dark. The hungry Scots fell on the town, Royalist as it was, and stripped it bare. The chase lasted till the 19th, when, at Winwick, Cromwell overtook them, killed 1000 and took 2000 prisoners. On the 20th he wrote from Warrington: "We have quite tired our horses in pursuit of the enemy. They are so tired and in such confusion, that if my horse could but trot after them I could take them all. This

is a glorious day : God help England to answer Aet. 49
His mercies." [1] On August 22 Hamilton capitu-
lated at Uttoxeter, and was taken to London to
die. The prisoners, amounting to 10,000, were a
terrible burden on Parliament. Most of them were
most unwilling soldiers who had been compelled
to enlist. They were liberated. The remainder
were shipped to Barbadoes and sold to planters,
or to Venice for the service of that Republic.
It was a crushing defeat to the friends of the king
and the enemies of England. Cromwell described it
in a letter to the House with a touch of awe : " I
could hardly tell how to say less, there being so
much of God in it; and I am not willing to say
more, lest there should seem to be any of man." [2]
It was the first battle of any magnitude in which
he had held the chief command; the enemy had
been three to one. He ended by urging Parliament to recognise the hand of God, and so to act
that " all that will live peaceably may have countenance, and they that are incapable and will not
leave troubling the land may speedily be destroyed
out of the land." It was a stern note that he
sounded. But there was no touch of vindictive-
ness. On September 30 Cromwell captured

[1] Carl. ii. 35.   [2] Carl. ii. 32.

1648 Berwick, and made for Edinburgh. The letters during that headlong campaign are full of strong religious workings, care for the widows of his fallen friends, and stern suppression of plunder. Across the Tweed a regiment raised in Durham "behaved themselves rudely, which as soon as the Lieutenant-General of this army had notice of, he caused it to rendezvous; and the Scottish people having challenged several horses taken from them by that regiment, the Lieutenant-General caused the said horses to be restored back, and the plunderers to be cashiered."[1] Even Hamilton, speaking of him at his own trial said, "Indeed he was so very courteous and so very civil as he performed more than he promised, and I must acknowledge his favour to those poor wounded gentlemen that I left behind, that they were by him taken care of, and truly he performed more than he did capitulate for."[2] But he was unflinching in demanding the punishment of those who had brought this new war on the country. In his eyes they were murderers, and murderers flying in the face of God. There was no cruelty in his nature. "Temper exceeding fiery as I have known," said one who knew him;[3] "yet the flame of it kept down for

---

[1] Carl. ii. 57.   [2] Gard. iv. 206.   [3] Carl. ii. 78.

most part or soon allayed; and naturally com- Aet. 49
passionate towards objects in distress, even to an
effeminate measure. Though God had made him
a heart wherein was left little room for any fear but
what was due to God Himself, yet did he exceed
in tenderness towards sufferers." And this temper
he maintained under terrible provocation. By
the end of October he had returned from Scotland,
and was encamped at Knottingley to reduce Pontefract and Scarborough, which still held out against
Parliament. On October 29 a party of Royalists
rode out of Pontefract and into Doncaster, where
they gained admission to Colonel Rainsborough's
lodging by saying that they brought a message
from Cromwell. They murdered him in cold blood,
and regained Pontefract in safety. This dastardly
deed more than any event of battles excited the
cry for blood in the hearts of the Independents.
To them this and all such deeds lay at the door of
"that man of blood, Charles Stuart." It was a
week after this that Cromwell wrote to Robert
Hammond who had charge of Charles at Carisbrooke, warning him against any attempt to
negotiate with the king. "How easy to take
offence at things called Levellers, and run into an
extremity on the other hand, meddling with an

1648 accursed thing. Peace is only good when we receive it out of our Father's hand, and most dangerous to go against the will of God to attain it."

No, the cup of indignation against the king and his duplicity was almost full. Prince Rupert was now in command of the fleet, and Charles, having wrecked what was known as the Treaty of Newport in September by his incurable insincerity, was busy in communications with Ormond in Ireland, bidding him act, while prepared to disavow him, writing "be not startled at my great concessions concerning Ireland, for that they will come to nothing." [1] The army, led by Ireton, made overtures to Charles which anticipated in all essential points the constitutional system of the present day. The king pretended to listen, and even gave the commissioners a letter ordering Ormond to desist from the very action which in private he had commanded. The only hope for the king was to grant terms which would bind his own hands, and render him in his own eyes no longer a king. A sovereign like our own reigning in the affection and the judgment of a whole nation just because the prerogative had been

[1] Gard. *Civil War*, iv. 225.

surrendered, and the supreme authority of the Aet. 49
people admitted, never came within the range of
his vision. His understanding could not grasp
such a situation. His conscience would not have
allowed it.

The letters from Knottingley grow sterner and
sterner. One mind, in that prolonged siege of
Pontefract, which did not end till March 22, is
revolving the great question, and arriving at a
clear decision. "We are sure the goodwill of
Him who dwelt in the Bush has shined upon us;
and we can humbly say, we know in whom we
have believed, who can and will perfect what
remaineth." [1]

He exhorts Hammond to consider "the chain
of Providence whereby God brought him" to
Carisbrooke "and that person" (the king), to him.
The king must not escape. The army is a lawful
power called by God to oppose and fight against
the king. "Let us look into Providences.
Malice, sworn malice, against God's people, now
called saints, to root out their name; and yet
they getting arms, and therein blessed with
defence and more!" In this army an increasing
number are coming over to the idea of resistance

[1] Carl. iv. 82.

F

1648 to the death.   What good can come from the king!   "Good by this man, against whom the Lord hath witnessed; and whom thou knowest!" Impossible.

What a perilous suggestion it sounds, that the army should claim to be the instrument of God, and count its own impulses as the revelation of His will!   But it must be remembered that Cromwell would never have claimed this for an ordinary army.   It was this army, which he knew, filled with men of faith and prayer, signally blessed in what seemed an impossible undertaking, an army as exceptional for an army as he himself was for a general, that began to appear to him, in the long waiting before Pontefract, a chosen instrument to strike down a royal head.

If our eyes are turned away from the peril of the nation to the personal conduct of the king, our sympathies are sure to be overborne.   All the good qualities of the royal captive stand clearly out in the last two months of his life.   On November 25 a warrant was issued by Parliament "that the person of the king be proceeded against in the way of justice."   But Hammond, in spite of all Cromwell's letters, had not the

temerity to touch the Lord's anointed. He was Aet. 49
replaced by Ewer. The king's personal attendants
urged him to make another attempt at escape.
With great dignity he replied, "They have promised me, and I have promised them, and I
will not break first." He was reminded that the
promise had been given to the House and not to
the army. "Never let that trouble you," he
replied; "I would not break my word to prevent
it." Evasion or equivocation had been his constant practice for years. But in the keen air of
approaching death he fell back on the honour
which refuses to utter a lie. On December 1
the king was removed to Hurst Castle. The
army, led by such spirits as Harrison, had fully
determined to bring the king to what it considered
justice. On the 2nd it marched into London,
and Fairfax took up his quarters at Whitehall.
The House, on the other hand, was eager for
delay, and still clung to the idea of a settlement
on the lines of the Treaty of Newport. If the
purpose of the army was to be carried out, Parliament would have to be coerced. Ireton and
Harrison pleaded for a dissolution. The existing
House, they said, had forfeited its trust. What
was needed was a new and free representative.

1648 This was the plea of a doctrinaire constitution-
alism. If it had prevailed, the fruits of the war
would inevitably have been lost. The council of
the army decided, therefore, for the unprecedented
and unconstitutional method of " purging " Parliament. On December 6, without authority from
Fairfax or Cromwell, who only arrived from
Pontefract on the evening of that day, the House
of Commons was beset with soldiers early in the
morning. As the members assembled, Lord Grey
of Groby, himself a member, pointed out to Colonel
Pride those who were holding out against the wish
of the army. One hundred and forty-three
members were turned back from the House, and
forty-one who resisted were lodged in confinement.
When Cromwell reached London in the evening,
he was informed of what had been done, and said,
that though he had not been acquainted with this
design he was glad of it, and would endeavour to
maintain it.

Knowing the issue of this violent procedure as
we do, it is difficult for us to do justice to the
thoughts that were moving in such minds as
Harrison's and Cromwell's. It is quite certain
that at this time Cromwell at least had no idea of
putting the king to death. But he was quite

resolved that he must be dethroned. If the en- Aet. 49
feebled Parliament of 1640 could not face that
dread necessity, the victorious army of 1645 and
1647 must do it. It was intolerable that one shifty
and untrustworthy man should be able to keep
the country in perpetual unrest, and by his own
schemes, or by the efforts of his queen, his son,
his nephew Rupert abroad, his fanatical followers
in Scotland, or his devoted lieutenant in Ireland,
to plunge England into new wars year after year.
Without any personal antipathy to Charles, Cromwell saw, what now every student of history can
see, with his secret correspondence and his endless
duplicities laid bare, that so long as this king
reigned or had any hope of reigning, there could
be no peace for the country without the sacrifice
of that which was dearer than peace, that for
which the nation had originally taken up arms and
striven at infinite cost through these seven years,—
liberty. Strictly speaking, there was no constitutional method of saving England, or of gaining
that freedom which was to be her dearest
possession. These victorious soldiers had to
decide whether they would see her fetters re-
imposed or save her unconstitutionally. They
chose the latter alternative. It is not for us who

1648 benefit by their desperate course to blame the men who, to carry it out, took their lives in their hands, and incurred the execration of mankind.

A few days before Christmas the king was brought up to Windsor by Harrison, who, as Charles confessed, "looked like a soldier, and having some judgment in faces, if he had observed him so well before he should not have harboured that ill opinion of him."[1] Just before his arrival at Windsor a fleet horse had been provided by the anxious care of a Royalist, to enable the king to escape. But the horse fell lame. The verdict had gone forth. No power on earth, no favourable accident, no intercession of love or mercy, could save the doomed king.

In the council of officers Ireton urged that the king should be brought to trial and then committed to prison till he consented "to abandon his negative voice" on measures passed by Parliament, "to part from Church lands, and to abjure the Scots." Cromwell advocated a more cautious course still. Let them, he said, defer the king's trial and proceed with the subjects, such as Norwich and Capel, who were responsible for the late war. There is a remarkable letter extant

[1] Gard. *Civil War*, iv. 280.

written by a Royalist on December 21, which Aet. 49
asserts that Cromwell was opposing the extremists
in the Council, and only gave countenance to the
cry of the Levellers for justice on the king in
order to elicit their wicked principles and inten-
tions, with the view of frustrating them. This
writer credits Cromwell with the view that it
would be irrational to " exchange a king in their
power for one out of their power ; " that is, Charles
I. for Charles II., " potent in foreign alliances and
strong in the affections of the people." [1]

Indeed, we find Cromwell in urgent consultation
with Sir Bulstrode Whitlocke and Sir Thomas
Widdrington, the two legal commissioners for the
custody of the great seal, during the next few
days, trying to find a basis of agreement between
the army and the House, on which the king's life
could be secured. And on Christmas Day, in
the council of officers, it is admitted by a hostile
Royalist newspaper that he pleaded with them to
spare the king's life as a matter of policy, on his
acceptance of the conditions which were then
being offered to him.

But two days later the king had absolutely
rejected these conditions which had been carried

[1] Gard. *Civil War*, iv. 282.

1649 to him at Windsor by Lord Denbigh. Charles
preferred to die, if he might not be what he himself considered a king. To renounce the negative
voice, to accept the position which Queen Victoria
holds to-day, seemed to him the surrender of his
kingship. That was the whole tragedy of the
situation. England required a constitutional
Monarchy. She had risen in arms and poured
out her blood and treasure to secure it. Her
unhappy king was in principle opposed to such a
monarchy. He refused to be such a monarch.
It is no exaggeration to say that he signed his
own death - warrant. There is much that is
admirable in this obstinacy. To forfeit his own
indefeasible sovereignty seemed to him treachery
not only to himself but to his descendants; nor
had he sufficient knowledge of the English Constitution to understand that the sovereignty of the
throne had always been implicitly limited by
checks in the interest of the people. To surrender
the property of the bishops was to him not only
ingratitude to the best supporters of his prerogative, but sacrilege committed against God. It is
possible and even easy to sympathise with this
pathetic king at this crisis of his fate. But we
have followed the story so far in vain if we do

not recognise that the judgment of God had gone
out against the whole conception for which
Charles was standing, and that Cromwell would
have been untrue, not only to his own conscience,
but to his country and her future, to his God and
His amazing manifestations, if he had permitted
pity for the king to arrest him in the task which
he was appointed to discharge.

Cromwell had done everything in his power,
that was not inconsistent with the supreme purpose of the long struggle, to save the king. All
efforts had failed. Even Vane, who had held out
against any suggestion of condemning the king
to death, was obliged to give way. On January 1, 1649, the House of Commons passed an
Ordinance instituting a special court for the trial
of the king, and sent it to the Lords with the
resolution that " by the fundamental laws of this
kingdom it is treason in the king of England for
the time being to levy war against the Parliament
and kingdom of England." It was a new definition of treason, but a definition which would
stand ; by the audacious action which Parliament
was now meditating it would in future be treason
for an English king to levy war against his own
people, as represented in Parliament. Three

1649 judges were named, who were to sit with 150 commissioners to form the court. Cromwell, speaking on this Ordinance before it left the Commons, is reported to have said : " If any man whatsoever hath carried on the design of deposing the king, and disinheriting his posterity, or if any man had yet such a design, he should be the greatest traitor and rebel in the world; but since the providence of God hath cast this upon us, I cannot but submit to Providence, though I am not yet provided to give you advice." [1]

That sounds strange and even " hypocritical " language from one who in the course of that same month was to sit on the Commission and relentlessly bring his king to the block. But Cromwell's was a mind which did not form distant plans. His notion of waiting upon God and watching for His signs forbade it. " No man rises so high," he is reported to have said, " as he who sees not whither he is going." He saw those directions of Providence not in his own speculations but in the concrete facts which were before his eyes. Even Professor Gardiner is surely severe on him in saying that " the reference to Providence was with Cromwell an infallible

[1] Gard. *Civil War*, iv. 288.

indication of a political change of front." [1] His Aet. 50
firm conviction was that God guides those who
trust in Him. He frankly accepted events as
God's guidance. To him Marston Moor and
Naseby decided against the Royalist cause, and
Preston decided against the Scotch intervention.
This was the voice of God to him. His whole
soul was set on saving Charles, as we have seen.
But the refusal of the king to accept the minimum
terms was, in Cromwell's eyes, the refusal of
Charles to be saved, and the handwriting of God
going out against him. The bewildered cry in
the words before us is the expression of a surprise
which overwhelmed the speaker, as he began to
see in what direction the finger of God was pointing. He would save the king; God would not;
who was he to fight against God?

The House of Lords refused the Ordinance.
Apparently the judges declined to serve. On
January 6, an Act was finally passed by the House
of Commons creating a High Court of Justice
composed of 135 members for the trial of the
king. In the discussion which preceded the
passing of the Act, some notable principles were
laid down—*e.g.* "The people are, under God,

[1] Gard. *Civil War*, iv. 288.

1649 the original of all just power"; "The Commons of England, in Parliament assembled, being chosen by and representing the people, have the supreme power in this nation"; "Whatsoever is enacted or declared for law by the Commons hath the force of law, although the consent and concurrence of king or House of Peers be not had thereto."

The preamble of the Act itself, which expresses precisely the thought of Cromwell, gives in few words the whole indictment against the king: "Not content with those many encroachments which his predecessors had made upon the people in their rights and freedoms, he had a wicked design totally to subvert the ancient and fundamental laws and liberties of his nation, and in their place to introduce an arbitrary and tyrannical government; and besides all other evil ways and means to bring this design to pass, he hath prosecuted it with fire and sword, levied and maintained a cruel war in the land against the Parliament and kingdom, whereby the country hath been miserably wasted, the public treasure exhausted, trade decayed, thousands of people murdered, and infinite other mischiefs committed; for all which high and treasonable offences Charles Stuart might long since justly have been brought to

exemplary and condign punishment. Whereas Aet. 50
also the Parliament, well hoping that the restraint
and imprisonment of his person, after it had
pleased God to deliver him into their hands,
would have quieted the distempers of the
kingdom, did forbear to proceed judicially against
him, but found by sad experience that such their
remissness served only to encourage him and his
accomplices in the continuance of their evil
practices, and in raising of new commotion,
rebellions, and invasions; for the prevention,
therefore, of the like or greater inconveniences,
and to the end no chief officer or magistrate
whatever may hereafter presume traitorously and
maliciously to imagine or contrive the enslaving
or destroying of the English nation, and to expect
impunity for so doing, this court is appointed for
the hearing, trying, and adjudging the said Charles
Stuart."

Impossible as it was to give a constitutional
colour to this proceeding, it is equally impossible
to deny that the whole of this charge, with the
exception of the wicked motive attributed to the
unhappy king, was literally true. Before the bar
of constitutional law the whole process is an out-
rage, a nightmare of rebellion and wickedness.

1649 Before the bar of national equity, and in the
presence of that spirit of liberty which presides
over the progress of history, and has been the
peculiar guardian and promoter of our country's
welfare, the indictment was incisively accurate,
and the high-handed method of pressing it home
and confirming its verdict was the only one available.   And as Cromwell was the strong nerve, the
unflinching will, in the whole of this terrible drama,
we can understand how Constitutionalists and
Royalists have regarded him with holy horror,
while lovers of liberty and pioneers of democracy
have seen in him the inflexible servant of God who
bare not the sword in vain, an instrument in the
hand of God for effecting one of the most critical
advances in political and religious development.

What fills the student to-day with wonder is
the amazing courage of the men who grasped this
abstract principle of equity, and ventured to carry
it into practice in the face of a nation stupefied
with astonishment, and of Europe speechless with
horror.   Even the bravest might have trembled.
On January 8 the court met in the Painted
Chamber.   Only fifty-two appeared.   Fairfax was
there, the first and last sitting at which he was
present.   But Cromwell and Ireton and the

famous colonels of the New Model were there, Aet. 50
with several of the members of the House, in-
cluding Lord Grey of Groby, Ludlow, Marten, and
Hutchinson; and they were in no mood to flinch.
An adjournment was necessary. And next day
the Lords tried to arrest proceedings by moving
that any king who in the future should do what
Charles had done should be brought to trial.
But the mind of the strong men in the Commons
was fully made up. A thousand dangers waited
on delay. It was the strength of Royalist feeling
even in breasts which were not Royalist that made
it imperative to act quickly.[1] It was the obvious
shrinking of even such staunch men as Fairfax
from bringing the king to trial at all, that convinced the stalwarts that nothing would avail but
to bring him to the block. On January 10 the
court chose Serjeant Bradshaw as its president.
On the 17th the king was lodged in Cotton House.
It is said that Cromwell, watching him from his
window in Whitehall, reminded his fellow-com-
missioners that if Charles should demand by what

[1] See the story afterwards told by Algernon Sidney.
He had objected to Cromwell, "first, the king can be
tried by no court, secondly, no man can be tried by this
court." Cromwell replied, "I tell you we will cut off his
head with the crown upon it" (Gard. *Civil War*, iv. 296).

1649 authority they sat, they must be ready with an
answer. What should it be ? No one knew
better than he the illegality of the whole position ; but no one was ever more convinced of the
absolute justice and righteousness in God's sight
of a daring action. After a silence Marten made
the memorable answer, " In the name of the
Commons in Parliament assembled, and all the
good people of England."

On January 20 this extraordinary court met
in Westminster Hall. Bradshaw, in the shot-
proof hat still preserved at Oxford, sat with
the commissioners on a dais at the southern end
of the hall. In the two corners were galleries
provided for ladies and other distinguished spec-
tators. The king was placed on a chair covered
with crimson velvet in face of his judges. Behind
were a large number of soldiers under Colonel
Axtell. The public was freely admitted to the
rest of the huge space. The roll of the judges
was called. To the name of Fairfax, a voice
answered from the gallery, " He has more wit
than to be here ; " it came from Lady Fairfax, a
strong Presbyterian. Sixty-eight answered to
their names. Then John Cook, the solicitor of
the Commonwealth, read the indictment. To the

general charge was added that Charles was the Aet. 50 author of the Second Civil War and of the revolt of the fleet, and had issued commissions to the prince and other rebels and foreigners, and also to Ormond and to the Irish rebels and revolters associated with him. On these grounds the Commonwealth impeached him as "a tyrant, traitor, murderer, and a public and implacable enemy." While Cook was speaking, the king attempted to stop him by reaching out his stick, but "the head of his staff happened to fall off, at which he wondered; and seeing none to take it up, he stooped for it himself." When the word "traitor" was mentioned, he burst into a laugh.

Bradshaw called on the king to answer, "in the behalf of the Commons assembled in Parliament and the good people of England." Once more Lady Fairfax raised her voice: "It is a lie, not half nor a quarter of the people of England. Oliver Cromwell is a traitor." Axtell ordered his men to fire into the gallery, an order which they happily disobeyed; and the talkative lady was removed.

The king asked by what authority he had been brought to that bar. He was, he said, king by inheritance and not by election. To answer,

1649 except to lawful authorities, would be to betray
his trust and the liberties of his people. In a
word he defied the court and refused to plead.
As he was removed to Cotton House, the soldiers
cried " Justice ! Justice !" Other voices in the hall
cried " God save the king."

On the 22nd the king took up a still more
defiant attitude. He was devoid of fear, and not
anxious to save his life. " It is not," he said,
" my case alone ; it is the freedom and liberty of
the people of England ; and do you pretend what
you will, I stand more for their liberties ; for, if
power without law may make laws, may alter the
fundamental laws of the kingdom, I do not know
what subject there is in England that can be sure
of his life, or anything that he calls his own."

The next day the prisoner still more decisively
refused to plead.

Charles had the law on his side, and the
English people are always in the main on the side
of law. A few criminals defy it. A few idealists
see a better law beyond and strive towards it.
And here was a handful of men who saw that by
law England could be enslaved, or plunged into
endless tumults and divisions, while beyond they
beheld the fair vision of a free Commonwealth

governed by a constitutional monarch. If that Aet. 50
was to be realised, *law* must be broken. All the
conservative instincts of England were rallying
against the court and the trial. The Presbyterians were opposed to it, and their pulpits were
denouncing its iniquity. Scottish commissioners
arrived in London to deliver their protest. Under
the leadership of Argyle the northern Parliament
declared against the trial. Whether out of love
for their native king, or out of hate for the Independents and their resolute predominance, Scotland as a whole, no longer merely a Royalist party,
was rallying round the throne. Ireland, Catholic
and Presbyterian, was unanimous for the king.
With the Scotch commissioners Cromwell attempted to reason. He urged that a breach of
trust in the king ought to be punished more than
any crime whatsoever. He reminded them that
by their Covenant they swore to defend the king's
person in defence of the true religion; but it was
the king who was the great hindrance to the
settlement of true religion. Further, their Covenant bound them to bring all incendiaries, malignants and enemies of the cause to punishment.
The king was the authority under whose commission all the malignants under Montrose, for

1649 instance, had acted. Such arguments were in-
effectual in persuading the Scots, but they show
how absolutely persuaded Cromwell was himself.
The king was guilty of a capital breach of trust,
and he had engaged in a calculated design to
suppress the true religion.

On January 25 the court had reached the decision to proceed to sentence against the king,
as a traitor, " and that this condemnation shall
extend to death." On the next day they formu-
lated the sentence of high treason, and decided
that he should be put to death by the severing of
his head from his body. On Saturday the 27th
the king was summoned to hear his sentence read.
Sixty-seven commissioners were present in Westminster Hall; and, amid loud cries of " Justice !
Justice !" the president, Bradshaw, proceeded to
say that, upon the contumacy of the prisoner and
the notoriety of the fact, the court had agreed
upon a sentence, but that as the prisoner had
expressed a wish to be heard, it was ready to
listen to him, provided that he did not question
its jurisdiction. Charles replied by appealing
from the court to the Lords and Commons assembled in the Painted Chamber. The court
considered this request for half an hour, and then

decided against it.   Bradshaw then made a long   Aet. 50
speech, citing the precedents of Edward II.,
Richard II., and Mary Queen of Scots, and showing that Charles had planned the destruction of
the realm.   Then the sentence was read.   Charles
wished to answer, but he was told that it was
too late.   He was led away protesting: "I am
not suffered to speak; expect what justice other
people will have."

For two days efforts were made to resist the
execution of the sentence by the Assembly of
Divines, by two Dutch Ambassadors, even by
Fairfax, and by the Prince of Wales, who sent a
blank paper to Parliament inviting them to
make what terms they pleased if they would only
spare his father.   Undoubtedly, the vast majority
of England would have joined in these protests.
Cromwell thought otherwise.   Not lightly or
quickly, but with strong agonies of thought and
prayer, had he come to the fatal decision.   To
recede from it would have been in his eyes to
have disobeyed God from fear of man.   His
resolute will secured the reluctant signatures
of fifty-nine of the commissioners to the death-
warrant.

At two o'clock on January 30, before the

1649 Palace of Whitehall, where Cromwell was lodging, the king met his doom with exquisite grace and manly dignity. On the scaffold he reiterated the very convictions which made his death necessary. As for the people, he said, he desired their liberties, which consisted in *being* governed. "It is not their having a share in the government; that is nothing appertaining unto them. A subject and a sovereign are clean different things; and, therefore, until you do that—I mean that you put the people in that liberty—they will never enjoy themselves."

It is in this last confession of the king's, at the very moment of his death, that Cromwell's justification is to be found. If Cromwell had hesitated or flinched, that ruinous doctrine of Charles the First might have prevailed, and England to-day might have been in the condition of Russia. No Royalist in England felt more keenly the anguish of the deed than the man whose stern will, acting as he believed at the bidding of God, had been the main instrument in perpetrating it. That night the dead king lay in the Banqueting House at Whitehall; and two faithful watchers saw a muffled figure enter, approach the body, and look at it attentively;

then they heard the words sighed out " Cruel
necessity!"   It was always believed that the
muffled figure was that of Oliver Cromwell; and
it is quite certain that the words expressed his
view of the tragical event.

Aet. 50

CHAPTER V

THE COMMONWEALTH

1649

"It matters not who is our commander-in-chief if God be so."—CROMWELL.

1649 NOTHING is clearer than that Cromwell never had any qualms of conscience about the execution which has branded him with the name of traitor and murderer. It chances that we have a letter from him written on February 1, two days after that terrible scene. It is addressed to his "very loving friend Mr. Robinson, preacher at Southampton," and it is occupied with a negotiation for the marriage of his son Richard to the daughter of Mr. Mayor:—"Upon your testimony of the gentlewoman's worth, and the common report of the piety of the family, I shall be willing to entertain the renewing of the motion upon such conditions

as may be to mutual satisfaction. Only I think Aet. 50
that a speedy resolution will be very convenient
to both parties. The Lord direct all to His glory.
I desire your prayers therein." The resolution
was not very speedy. It was only on April 15,
when very serious affairs were pending, and after
many letters, that the two fathers had come to
some agreement, and the marriage was celebrated
on May-day. But this quiet domestic transaction
shows the state of Cromwell's mind. There is no
reason to think that he was more disturbed than
a judge would be who has passed sentence on a
criminal. And clearly nothing was further from
his thought than that he by the movement of
events would be thrust into the royal place which
his unflinching purpose had rendered vacant.

On February 5 Charles II. was proclaimed in
Scotland and Montrose was nominated to command
for the new king in the North. Scottish commissioners were despatched to the Hague where
the prince held his court, and they cherished the
futile faith that they would induce him to sign
the Covenant, which was not in itself difficult, and
to carry it out in his reign, which was absolutely
impossible. In Ireland, on the other hand, the
cause of King Charles was supported by Ormond,

1649 who granted to the Irish a parliament of their own, and promised liberty for the Catholic religion. Charles was invited to appear in Ireland. The Queen of Bohemia sold her jewels to man his fleet; and Prince Rupert sailed to Kinsale with eleven ships.

The men, on the other hand, who had brought King Charles to the block were not disposed to hand over the government of England to his son. They were prepared to crush the new Royalists in Ireland and in Scotland, and to make a complete work of the great task which they had begun. The first thought was to create a strong navy to intercept foreign invaders, and under Topham, Blake, and Deane, England, the England of the Commonwealth, began for the first time to challenge the place of the leading sea-power in Europe.

Within a fortnight after the execution of the king Parliament nominated a Council of State, to wield the executive power. There were forty-one members. For the moment Cromwell was made president. But the inconvenience of having a general, who must again soon be on active service, as its head, was at once apparent. And Bradshaw, the president of the High Court of Justice, was appointed as president of the Council. This was on March 10. There was not likely to be much Aet. 50 difficulty in carrying on the Government under such an arrangement. But the hands of the Council and Parliament were soon sufficiently full. John Lilburne, restless doctrinaire, put himself at the head of those in the army, and out of it, who were eager for a Republican settlement. Under the title of *England's New Chains,* he published a protest against the Council, and demanded that military commanders—he was pointing at Cromwell, Ireton, and Fairfax who had been admitted to Parliament—should not be allowed to sit in the House. Cromwell had much sympathy with this fiery spirit, and had more than once thrown his ægis over the man and saved him from himself. But it was no time for constitutional debates. Stern work had to be done. And when certain troopers, roused by Lilburne, came to the House to present the petition of the army, they were promptly cashiered. Cromwell, as usual, saw the rigid fact, and laid aside mere sentiment. " You have no other way," he said, " to deal with these men but to break them, or they will break you."

Equally resolute was he that Hamilton and Lord Capel, who, alas ! had been first of all in this Parliament to complain of grievances, and Holland

1649 and Poyer, should die for their share in kindling that unpardonable Second Civil War in Wales and in the North. It was intolerable to him that the chief delinquent should suffer, and not those who had been his commissioned agents and his prime abettors. The first three died nobly in Palace-Yard. As for Poyer, lots were drawn between him and his two confederates Powel and Langharne. He was shot in Covent Garden.

A week later, March 17, Acts were formally passed through Parliament abolishing the office of king, and also the House of Lords. In this way the decks were cleared for action. Trouble was brewing in Ireland. Presbyterian Inchiquin was uniting with Ormond; and Michael Jones, a fine specimen of the militant Puritan, was holding out for Parliament in Dublin, with small chance of success unless effectual succour were forthcoming. Accordingly, on March 15, Cromwell was invited to take the command in Ireland, and on that same day John Milton was appointed as " Secretary for the Foreign Languages " in the Council of State. " It matters not who is our commander-in-chief if God be so," was the remark with which Cromwell received his appointment. But he plainly recognised the call of God in the appointment. In

his heart there burned a hot fire of anger against Aet. 50
the Papal Irish. Doubtless he had read in May's
History of Parliament, published two years before,
those awful words:[1] "The innocent Protestants
were on a sudden deprived of their estates, and the
persons of above 200,000 men, women, and children
murdered, many of them with exquisite tortures
within the space of one month." It is evident
that Cromwell went to Ireland in a mood very
different from that in which he approached his
previous military tasks. He was conscious to
himself of carrying an avenging sword. He had
no opportunity of forming a correct judgment
about the Irish question. But the blood of those
slaughtered Protestants cried to him from the
ground. And with Hyde at the Hague denouncing,
and demanding the restoration of the monarchy
just as it had been before the war, and with
Catholic Ireland throwing open her ports to welcome
the new king's ships, and fortifying her towns to
resist the authority of Parliament, he immediately
recognised that for the cause which he had at
heart there was no more necessary battlefield than
that across the Irish Channel.

But there was a melancholy piece of work to be

[1] Lib. ii. 4.

1649 done before the Irish campaign could be attempted.
The troops—the redoubtable New Model itself—
were in an effervescence of Republican mutiny.
Scrope's regiment, which had advanced as far as
Salisbury on the way to Ireland, refused to leave
England until the liberties of the country were
secured, that meant until the Long Parliament
had consented to dissolve, and to summon a new
representative of the people.   Most of Ireton's
regiment, the troops quartered round Bristol, and
Harrison's and Skippon's men, were of the same
opinion.[1]   On May 6 an old corporal, William
Thompson, collected a local force of the discon-
tented at Banbury.   He was inflamed by Lilburne's
burning rhetoric.   He was shot at Wellingborough
a few days later.   But affairs wore a serious aspect
when, on the 9th, Fairfax and Cromwell reviewed
their own troops in Hyde Park.   The Lieutenant-
General addressed the men, reminded them of
what Parliament had done in punishing delinquents,
assured them that it had on April 15 resolved to
dissolve and to assemble a new Parliament, though
a new constitution could not easily be framed at a
moment of peril like the present, and induced
them to take the sea-green ribbons out of their

[1] Gard. *History of Commonwealth*, i. 54.

hats, which had been assumed as the badge of Aet. 50 discontent. On the 12th it was necessary to commit Lilburne to the Tower. That same day Fairfax and Cromwell were at Alton, and joined by Scrope, who informed them that there were 600 mutineers in arms. The generals had the greatest sympathy and consideration for these men, whose revolt was one of principle. It was indeed the inevitable result of enlisting an army with ideas, men who had a political object in view which seemed to them of more importance than military obedience. A message was sent to them; and "let them know," said Cromwell, "that though we have sent messengers to them we will not follow with force at their heels." At Burford the mutineers were surprised and quickly surrendered.[1] The greater part of them were quietly restored to the ranks. Only two corporals, besides Thompson, suffered death.

It was a pleasant conclusion to this painful

[1] The famous scene in the churchyard at Burford is one of the most impressive and dramatic of the whole war; the ringleaders are drawn out for execution; three are shot, then the slaughter is stayed, the Lieutenant-General rises in the pulpit and pours out such a homily, that with tears and groans the mutinous troopers return to duty. In suppressing mutiny, Cromwell is always at his best (Frederic Harrison, *Life*, p. 135).

1649 episode, that on the 17th Fairfax and Cromwell
visited Oxford, where they received the honorary
degree of D.C.L., while Harrison, and some
other of the New Model colonels, were made
honorary Masters of Arts.   The Puritan University
well understood that the cause of order and settlement was in the hands of these inflexible soldiers;
and possibly the divines who now had the direction of affairs in the University perceived better
than subsequent unsympathetic generations have
done, that never was the sword borne more
valiantly or with a more pathetic desire for peace.
Doctor of Civil Law does not seem a very suitable
degree for a man who was passing to the most
sanguinary task of his life.   But the incongruity
was only in appearance.   Oxford never had a
worthier Doctor of Civil Law than Oliver
Cromwell.

It was two days later, May 19, that the Act
was passed through the House of Commons which
has a much deeper significance than any one at
the time understood.   " Be it declared and enacted
by this present Parliament, and by the authority
of the same, That the people of England, and of
all the dominions and territories thereunto
belonging, are, and shall be, and are hereby con-

stituted, made, established, and confirmed to be, Aet. 49
A COMMONWEALTH OR FREE STATE, and shall
from henceforth be governed as a Commonwealth
and Free State, by the supreme authority of this
nation the representatives of the people in Parliament, and by such as they shall appoint and
constitute officers and ministers under them for
the good of the people, and that without any King
or House of Lords." [1]

Constitutional historians of Saxon times, like
Professor Freeman, have delighted to show how
this idea was latent in the primitive Teutonic
institutions, and was never lost in the days before
the Norman Conquest. From the Conquest to
the time of the Tudors, the constant, though often
blind effort of the national life was to reassert
this essential idea. The Tudor and Stuart
autocracies were episodes, the one brilliant, the
other disastrous, in the constitutional development; and that deed of violence, the execution of
a king, was perhaps a "cruel necessity" in order
to dismiss the episodes and resume the proper line
of advance. The statesmen, therefore, who
asserted the fundamental principle of the Commonwealth, and the stern men of action who by their

[1] Carl. ii. 96.

H

1649 prowess gave it a momentary existence, were more truly in the main stream of the national life than those whom they had vanquished. Enjoying our own liberties and possibilities of progress to-day, we trace our descent back to Simon de Montfort, and to the Witenagemot, and to the Mark-system of our ancestors, not through Charles I. or Queen Elizabeth, but through Oliver Cromwell and the Independents in what was scornfully called the Rump Parliament.

But the men were before their time; they were speaking to the nineteenth and the twentieth century not to the seventeenth. Their idea was in the air, supported by the masterful spirit of Cromwell and an army, the like of which had never before been seen, but not yet resting on the firm foundation of the nation's conviction and deliberate will. It was with difficulty that the City could be induced to proclaim the decision of Parliament. Alderman Chambers, who had been the first citizen to resist the illegal taxation of Charles, was among the first to refuse compliance with the orders of the Commonwealth. He and some others were deprived of their dignities. On June 7, however, the City received the Speaker of the House with royal honours, and the members

of Parliament drove in state to the reception. A Aet. 50
Royalist or a Leveller managed to remove the
linch-pin of Cromwell's coach, and it broke down in
the procession. But the City magnates presented
both Fairfax and Cromwell with some handsome
plate and a gift of money.

Cromwell was now only detained from the work
which was calling for him in Ireland by the determination to secure from Parliament the means to
pay his army before he embarked. But there was
one other stroke of business effected on June 9.
He had opposed the dissolution for which Vane
and other theorists were clamouring early in the
year, because of the obvious practical difficulty of
summoning a new Parliament just when the constitutional head of the State had been removed.
But when it was proposed to fill up the places of
excluded and delinquent members by co-optation,
a course by which more than a hundred new
members would be introduced without any reference to the national will, he moved the alternative
proposal that Parliament should adjourn for two
or three months, leaving the reins of Government
in the hands of the Council of State. It was
always his method to consult the immediately
practicable. Others were hampered with theories

1649 of what an ideal government should be. Cromwell had no such embarrassment. He saw with
perfect clearness what must be done, and that once
seen he made for it by the most direct means.
The Council of State could be trusted. It consisted of godly men who were loyal to the Commonwealth. And for the business in hand, the
subjugation of this rebellious Ireland, and a
decisive settlement of these troublesome Scotch,
who were rallying under their Covenant king to
harass the Commonwealth, the Council would be
more serviceable than any Parliament. For the
present therefore he was well pleased to have
Parliament suspended, and to know under whose
commands he was serving. On June 15 he was
appointed Commander-in-Chief and Governor of
Ireland; his son-in-law, Ireton, was made lieutenant-general. The only difficulty was the money;
but Parliament before adjourning charged £400,000
on the Excise, and authorised an immediate loan
of £150,000.

We are approaching the most painful and
difficult chapter in Cromwell's history. We are
not to excuse or apologise; but we are determined to understand how the matter appeared in
the eyes of the chief actor. Happily his own

declaration, issued in the following year, enables
us to form an opinion on this point with some
certainty. " If ever men were engaged in a
righteous cause in the world, this will scarce be a
second to it. We are come to ask an account of
the innocent blood which hath been shed; and to
endeavour to bring to an account, by the blessing
and presence of the Almighty, in whom alone is
our hope and strength, all who by appearing in
arms, seek to justify the same. We come to
break the power of a company of lawless rebels,
who having cast off the authority of England, live
as enemies of human society; whose principles,
the world hath experience, are to destroy and sub-
jugate all men not complying with them. We
come by the assistance of God, to hold forth and
maintain the lustre and glory of English liberty in
a nation where we have an undoubted right to do
it,—wherein the people of Ireland may equally
participate in all benefits; to use liberty and fortune
equally with Englishmen, if they keep out of arms."[1]

It is possible, no doubt, to dispute with Cromwell the justice of his view. But it is not possible
to deny that if this was the situation as it presented itself to his eyes, the whole course of his

[1] Carl. ii. 223.

1649 action in Ireland receives a justification. This was not a war with a civilised enemy—it was vengeance on murderers. Against Ireland as such he had no ill-will, but whoever appeared in arms there was the aider and abettor of murderers. It was, therefore, his intention from the first, while showing every consideration, and even a tender solicitude for the population of Ireland, to execute summary vengeance upon all whom he found *in arms.*

CHAPTER VI

IRELAND

1649–1650

WHEN Cromwell left London on July 10, in a
coach drawn by six grey Flanders mares, and preceded by a milk-white standard, he had a task
before him which might have made him despair
but for his unswerving faith in the justice of his
cause. Ormond and Inchiquin, with a force of
10,000 men, had invested Dublin, and Michael
Jones had to all appearance small hope of holding
out. Monk, who had made a three months' convention with the great Ulster leader, O'Neill, was
still in Dundalk. And Coote occupied Londonderry for the Parliament. Otherwise the whole of
Ireland, Papal, Episcopal, and Presbyterian, was in
insurrection against the Commonwealth, and
Ormond was urging Charles II. to come and estab-

1649 lish his throne in the island. On July 11
Inchiquin seized Drogheda, and 880 of the forces
within its walls went over to the conqueror. On
July 24 Dundalk surrendered to Inchiquin, and
a week later O'Neill, released from his convention
with Monk, was ready to co-operate with Ormond.
Derry and Dublin, these were the only points of
light, and Jones' men in Dublin were so little to be
relied on that numbers of them deserted to the
enemy.

It is characteristic of Cromwell that his last act
before leaving London was to write a letter to
Speaker Lenthall on behalf of John Lowry, his
fellow-member for Cambridge, whose affairs were
disturbed by his fidelity to his duties.[1] No man's
life was ever more crowded with these "little
unremembered acts of kindness." But good news
awaited him at Milford Haven. He writes "from
aboard the *John*, August 13," to his loving
brother Richard Mayor. Michael Jones had
broken out of Dublin, and with far inferior numbers had routed Ormond; though, alas! the stain
of these Irish wars already began to appear : he
had massacred all the deserters from his army
found with the enemy, not sparing his own nephew,

[1] Carl. ii. 130.

Eliot. "This is an astonishing mercy; so great Aet. 50
and seasonable that indeed we are like them that
dreamed. What can we say! The Lord fill our
souls with thankfulness, that our mouths may be
full of His praise, and our lives too. These things
seem to strengthen our faith and love, against
more difficult times." And by the same hand
he writes to Richard's wife : " As for the pleasures
of this life, and outward business, let them be
upon the bye. Be above all these things by faith
in Christ. . . . The Lord is very near, which we
see by His wonderful works, and therefore He
looks that we of this generation draw near to
Him."[1]

Two days later the General had crossed the
Irish sea and was in Dublin. The first thing was
to purge the army of dissolute and debauched men,
and to issue a stern declaration against robbery and
ill-usage and other "cruelties upon the country
people." Before we proceed to deal with those
in arms, we must take every precaution to secure
those who are *not.* All officers who do not carry
out this regulation are to be displaced. His own

[1] Carl. ii. 136. The postscript is also characteristic of
the fatherly heart. "I hear thou didst lately miscarry.
Prithee take heed of a coach by all means ; borrow thy
father's nag when thou intendest to go abroad."

1649 soldiers found guilty of violating this inexorable decree were promptly hanged. It ill became an army executing the will of God to be guilty of any injustice. He could, a year later, in answering a Papist manifesto which charged him with massacre and other violence, exclaim, "Give us an instance of one man since my coming into Ireland, not in arms, massacred, destroyed, or banished, concerning the massacre or the destruction of whom justice hath not been done, or endeavoured to be done."[1] And the best proof of the absolute order and justice maintained in Cromwell's army was this that the supplies of provisions were better than had ever been known in an Irish army before. While Ormond and Inchiquin, the defenders of Ireland, ran short, Cromwell, the invader, found no difficulty in this respect; for the country people crowded into the camp as to a good market, where sure prices were given and fair dealing enforced. These things must be borne in mind as we come to Drogheda and Wexford. They remind us how impossible it is to let the usual judgment on Cromwell in Ireland pass unchallenged. It may be true, as Professor Gardiner says, that "of the thoughts and feelings of Irishmen, Cromwell took

[1] Carl. ii. 221.

no heed,"[1] but, always excepting the rebels, as Aet. 50
he conceived them, found in arms, he treated the
Irish population with a justice and a mercy which
they have not always found under the enlightened
administration of the nineteenth century.

When the army was purged, the next step was
to march northwards against Drogheda, which
had been garrisoned with 2871 men, the flower of
Ormond's army. One regiment left behind by
Inchiquin was composed of Englishmen and
Protestants. The rest were Irish Catholics. It
would seem that many of the Protestants deserted
to Cromwell before the siege began. The
governor, Sir Arthur Aston, was a Catholic, who
had been governor of Oxford in 1644.

On September 3 Cromwell's army, 10,000
strong, was encamped before the southern gate of
Drogheda, where supplies could easily reach it
from the sea. Ormond was in no position, after his
defeat, to bring succour; O'Neill was unable to
come to the rescue from the North. On Monday
the 9th the batteries began to play; and Cromwell
sent Aston a summons to surrender the town to
the use of the Parliament of England. Aston
refused; and it must be remembered that by the

[1] *History of Commonwealth*, i. 140.

1649 laws of war, as then understood, when a fortified
town refused the summons of surrender the lives
of all found in arms after the assault were held to
be forfeit.[1]   On Tuesday a breach had been made
in the wall.   Aston, a brave and honourable
soldier, with insufficient ammunition, and no hope
of reinforcements, knew that he could not hold
out, and resolved to die at his post.   On
Wednesday, at 5 o'clock in the evening, three
regiments stormed through the breach; but they
were hurled back, and Colonel Castle was among
the killed.   It was only when Cromwell himself
leapt forward to lead the baffled storming-party
that the defenders were driven in.   Aston
retreated to Mill Mount, which rises just within
the walls, determined to sell his life as dearly as
possible; but the bulk of the garrison poured
pell-mell down the street and across the bridge,
to find shelter in the northern town.   It was the

[1] "If a city will make no peace with thee, but will
make war against thee, then thou shalt besiege it; and
when the Lord thy God delivereth it into thy hand, thou
shalt smite every male thereof with the edge of the
sword . . . thou shalt save alive nothing that breatheth"
(Deut. xx. 12, etc.)

   It must be remembered that Cromwell had not the
light which criticism has shed on such an oracle of God
as this.

desperate valour of Sir Arthur Aston that nettled Aet. 50
Cromwell. "The governor and divers considerable officers being there, our men getting up to
them were ordered by me to put them all to the
sword. And indeed being in the heat of action, I
forbade them to spare any that were in arms in
the town; and I think that night they put to the
sword about 2000 men; divers of the officers and
soldiers being fled over the bridge into the other
part of the town, where about 100 of them
possessed St. Peter's Church-steeple, some the
west gate, and others a strong round tower next
to the gate called St. Sunday's. These being
summoned to yield to mercy, refused. Where-
upon I ordered the steeple of St. Peter's Church
to be fired, when one of them was heard to say in
the midst of the flames, 'God damn me, God
confound me, I burn, I burn.'" [1]

But this was not all. A few who had taken
refuge in the towers, and there fired on Cromwell's

[1] "I believe it has always been understood that the
defenders of a fortress stormed have no claim to quarter ;
and the practice which prevailed during the last century
of surrendering a fortress when a breach was opened in
the body of the place, and the counter-scarp had been
blown up, was founded on this understanding" (Welling-
ton's despatch, February 3, 1820, quoted by Gardiner,
Commonwealth, i. 132.)

1649 men afterwards surrendered. The order was given that the officers should be " knocked on the head," and every tenth man of the soldiers shipped for the Barbadoes. Sir Edmund Verney was enticed from Cromwell's presence by a certain Roper who " ran him through with a tuck." Lieutenant Colonel Boyle was summoned from dinner by a soldier and immediately shot. Every friar in the town was knocked on the head ; and there is reason to fear that even some civilians were inadvertently killed in the dread work of vengeance. Professor Gardiner remarks that Cromwell was probably the only man in the victorious army who imagined that this signal punishment required any excuse at all. That is the great distinction of Cromwell. In the callousness of a prolonged civil war, and in the suppression of these gratuitous rebellions against the sovereignty of England and of the People, he preserved the self-control, and even the compassion, which few of us maintain unimpaired through our own quiet lives. The terrible severity at Drogheda was not the result of passion, but the calculated sternness of a judge who hopes by a striking example to prevent future delinquencies. The day after Drogheda was taken he hastened to use the fact as a warning to the garrison of Dundalk : " If you, being warned thereby, shall surrender your garrison to the use of the Parliament of England, which by this I summon you to do, you may thereby prevent effusion of blood." [1] And four days later, writing to the Council of State from Dublin, he expresses the conviction that the enemy being filled with terror will be prevented from a useless resistance, and thus " this bitterness will save much effusion of blood, through the goodness of God." [2] And this expectation was justified.   For Dundalk at once submitted without bloodshed, and when Trim was summoned " upon the news of Tredah (Drogheda) some Scots companies, brought to assist the Lord of Ormond, ran away, leaving their great guns behind them, which also we have possessed."   In his account to Parliament of the storming he says, evidently with deep conviction : " I am persuaded that this is a righteous judgment of God upon these barbarous wretches who have imbued their hands in so much innocent blood, and that it will tend to prevent the effusion of blood for the future, which are the satisfactory grounds to such actions, which otherwise cannot

[1] Carlyle, ii. 147.   [2] *Ibid.* 148.

1649 but work remorse and regret." However Cromwell's action may strike us in gentler times and under quieter conditions, it is quite certain that he himself had no qualms of conscience upon the subject. As a man, as a Christian, as a singularly sensitive and tender heart, he grieved over the " cruel necessities" of his hard day's work, but he never questioned that he was doing God's bidding. A judge may have troubled dreams the night after he has passed the death sentence on a criminal, but he does not question that he has done his duty. And this is just the spirit which breathes in all the despatches from Ireland.

In October, while Milton's *Eikonoclastes* was endeavouring to counteract the effect of the *Eikon Basilike* in England, Cromwell was pushing his victory in the South of Ireland; Venables and Coote were bringing the North into obedience to the Parliament. Wexford, the harbour of the privateers who were damaging English commerce, had unhappily not learnt the lesson of Drogheda. Many of the citizens were privateers. The Royalist commander of the place was Colonel Synott. Cromwell spent two or three days in writing letters to him, which have been preserved, using every endeavour to make him surrender.

The terms offered were: soldiers and non- Aet. 50
commissioned officers, quarter for life and leave to
go to their homes; commissioned officers quarter
for their lives, but to render themselves prisoners;
" and as for the inhabitants, I shall engage myself
that no violence shall be offered to their goods,
and that I shall protect the town from plunder." [1]
But before these terms reached the governor,
Captain Stafford treacherously surrendered the
castle to Cromwell. Indeed Inchiquin's troops,
and even 500 of the garrison of Ross were at the
same time deserting to the Parliamentary side,
as every day the Royalist cause became more
distinctly Papal. The forces against him were,
as Cromwell perceived, discomfited by their own
divisions, and by the intrinsic impossibility of
founding a stable throne on a combination of
Presbyterians and Romanists. When the guns of
Wexford Castle were turned against the town,
the garrison deserted the walls and sought for
refuge in the shipping of the harbour. The
besiegers rapidly scaled the deserted walls and
poured into the town, where barricades were
thrown up in the streets. Frenzied with hatred
to England the pirates and soldiers offered resist-

[1] Carl. ii. 168.

I

1649 ance behind the barricades.   It was, as Cromwell says in the great despatch of October 14, to Lenthall,[1] a kind of accident, quite beyond his design, and we may suspect, when the first rush was made, beyond his control.   The resistance was madness.   When the barricades were carried an indiscriminate slaughter ensued.   Down to the water's edge the vanquished were driven pell-mell, and many were thrust into the waves and drowned.   About 1500 perished.   Cromwell lost " not twenty from first to last of the siege."   A pirate city is never regarded with lenient eyes, and it is quite certain that the soldiers who wreaked the vengeance of England on Wexford were in their own eyes justified as much as any expedition which civilisation has fitted out against the lairs of the Algerines or of Tunis.   After the stern example of Drogheda, and the terrible " accident " of Wexford, Cromwell, with wonderful self-restraint, abandoned all idea of pushing severity any further.   His remaining five months in Ireland was marked by one success after another, but by no actions which even the bitterest critic could censure.   Ross fell with a plentiful effusion of letters, but without effusion of blood.   At the

[1] Carl. ii. 169.

end of December there was no place on the coast, Aet. 50
between Londonderry and Cape Clear, with the
exception of Waterford, which was not in Cromwell's hands. It was all in his eyes a succession
of miraculous interventions from God; and his
letters overflow with those expressions of awe and
wonder which are natural to one who is standing
still to see the salvation of God. "It's easy to
object to the glorious actings of God, if we look
too much upon instruments . . . these nine
years, what hath God wrought? Be not offended
at the manner; perhaps no other way was left."

In that month of December the Irish prelates
assembled at Clanmacnoise issued a great manifesto against Cromwell and for the king. "We
will as one entire and united body forward by our
counsel, action, and device the advancement of
'his majesty's rights.'" It is this document more
than any other which has fixed on Cromwell the
charge of cruelty in his Irish campaign; and it
was this document which now openly allied the
cause of the king with that of the Pope. Cromwell
sat down and composed a burning reply to this
manifesto, a declaration in which his heart seems
throbbing even to-day, and in which all the deep
and almost volcanic convictions of his mind

1650 struggle for expression. The breath of freedom is
in these pages. He protests against the false
distinction between " clergy and laity." He
exclaims, "Arbitrary powers men begin to be
weary of in kings and churches; their juggle
between them mutually to uphold civil and
ecclesiastical tyranny begins to be apparent. This
principle, that people are for kings and churches,
and saints are for the Pope or churchmen, as you
call them, begins to be exploded." It was the
new world straining to be born, the great dis-
coveries of the eighteenth, of the nineteenth, and
even of the twentieth centuries dawning vivid,
though obscured, in a powerful and believing
soul. This stirring appeal to the Irish people
against their tyrants was not without its effect.
Town after town fell into his hands. Ormond
was completely beaten, and the command of the
Irish passed into the hands of Bishop Macmahon.
In February 1650 Parliament was trying to
express its sense of Cromwell's services by voting
him " the use of the lodgings called the Cockpit,
of the Spring Garden, and St. James's House, and
the command of St. James's Park." [1] On March
22 the order for recall reached him. A harder

[1] Carl. ii. 233.

and far less congenial task awaited him in the
North, where the deluded Scotch were rallying
round their "covenanted king." It was not,
however, till May, after the capture of Clonmell,
that he actually left Ireland in the hands of his
son-in-law, Ireton. On the 31st he entered
London amid a tumult of salutation, admiration,
gratitude, and thanksgiving. "What a crowd
come out to see your lordship's triumph," said one.
"Yes, but if it was to see me hanged, how many
more would there be!" was his reply.

Even Clarendon admits that Ireland flourished
under the settlement which was effected by
Cromwell. The "curse of Cromwell," with which
the world has rung ever since, was simply that in
the fearful pressure of his crowded life he had no
opportunity to carry out his policy to its issue.[1]
His best justification is found in the words of his
latest historian: "In dealing with Ireland, as in
dealing with the king, he imposed an emphatic

---

[1] Mr. F. Harrison's remark that the massacre at
Drogheda "is one of those damning charges which the
Puritan theology has yet to answer at the bar of
humanity," is too oracular to be strictly just. Positivist
theology was not yet above the horizon ; but he has yet
to show that any theology then existing in Europe would
have shrunk from the deed.

1650 negative on a situation which had become intolerable. In England there was to be no kingship
without good faith. In Ireland there was to be
no meddling with English political life, no attempt
to constitute an independent government in the
hands of the enemies of the religion and institutions of England." [1]

[1] Gardiner, *History of the Commonwealth*, i. 177.

CHAPTER VII

DUNBAR AND WORCESTER

1650–1651

Thou on the neck of crowned fortune proud
  Hast reared God's trophies, and His work pursued ;
  While Darwen stream, with blood of Scots imbrued,
And Dunbar field, resounds thy praises loud,
  And Worcester's laureate wreath.

WHEN Cromwell turned his steps home, leaving 1650
his son-in-law, Ireton, to complete his work in
Ireland, it was, as has been said, to face a task
much more arduous and less congenial than the
stern vengeance on Irish Papists. The Levellers,
led by Lilburne, had singled him out as the main
obstacle to their impracticable plans. Lilburne,
in the previous summer, had been brought to trial
for sedition. He had been released, but his
pamphlet, "An Impeachment of High Treason
against Oliver Cromwell and his Son-in-law,

1650 Henry Ireton," was in circulation, sowing that rooted mistrust of Cromwell's designs which was to embitter the rest of his life and to prejudice his memory for 250 years. And, more painful than the honest spleen of these republican fanatics, Presbyterian Scotland had formed her hopeless alliance with Charles II., which to eyes like Cromwell's bore the aspect of delusion bordering on insanity. The Scotch Commissioners, on May 1, 1650, after prolonged negotiations, wrested from the king the Treaty of Breda, in which he professed to take the Covenant. The best comment on this unprincipled transaction is that at the same time he was appealing for help to Pope Innocent X. with a promise of toleration for Catholics if he regained his throne. He was equal to his father in shifty disregard of truth; but he had this advantage over Charles I., that, having no religious principles at all, he found no difficulty in pretending to be a Presbyterian. His ill-omened understanding with his Scottish subjects was marked by an event as disgraceful to him as Strafford's execution had been to his father. He consented to the execution of Montrose, the chivalrous and gallant upholder of the Stuart cause in Scotland. The great soldier

was hanged in Edinburgh on May 21, loyal to
the last. "A few more weeks of life would have
revealed to him a Charles who was neither great,
good, nor just, veiling his honour before the
Covenanting creed, and seeking to gain his ends
by walking in the crooked paths of deceit." [1]

Happy were those supporters of the Stuarts
who achieved an early death in their service, even
though it came through their master's treachery.
They at least had the satisfaction of dying with
their eyes on the "divinity which doth hedge a
king." They who served and survived had to
learn what kind of a king is sometimes hedged by
this divinity.

On June 27 Charles reached Scotland—a
covenanted king,—and the Scottish forces under
David Leslie, supported by the fervent, if deluded
faith of the Presbyterian clergy, were at his disposal, to destroy the Commonwealth and restore
him to his English throne.

It was a heart-breaking task for the men of the
Commonwealth to turn their swords against the
Scottish Presbyterians, by whose aid they had
obtained their victory over the late king and
established the present government. Fairfax had

[1] Gard., *Commonwealth*, i. 254.

1650 no heart in the service, and could not be induced
to take the command. He was Presbyterian in
sympathy. The most he could say was that if the
Scotch invaded England his sword would be at the
service of the State. The task was equally distasteful to Cromwell. But Cromwell had never
reckoned with life and duty on the basis of his
personal pleasure. Led by an inner light, and
solemnly regarding events as the dispensations of
God, he was free from those chills and hesita-
tions in the cause to which men like Fairfax were
always liable. He lived in prayer. He saw in
what passed before his eyes God's answer to his
prayers. To him it was a kind of unbelief to call
in question these divine decisions or to treat the
divine dispensations as if they were " events."
" Shall we after all these our prayers, fastings,
tears, expectations and solemn appeals, call these
bare *events?* The Lord pity you."[1] The Commonwealth was to him no less manifestly a creation of
God than the Jewish polity proclaimed on Sinai ;
and if friends or foes assailed it he was there to
adventure life itself in its defence. To the Presbyterians he could and did address the most tender
appeals. With all sincerity he could assure them

[1] Carl. iii. 67.

that he came to Scotland " to provoke to love and Aet. 51
good works, to faith in our Lord Jesus Christ, and
repentance from dead works." He could plead
with them on the ground of their common faith.
The tenderness of a woman steals into these solemn
adjurations to recognise God's hand and to
abandon a cause against which He had declared.
But with a sorrowful determination he would use
all the power at his disposal, and that military
instrument which God had put into his hand, to
frustrate an attempt based on hypocrisy, to restore
the levelled throne. As Carlyle justly observed,
Cromwell turned to this Scotch campaign, his
mind filled with the 110th Psalm, his heart resting on its solemn promises. Never was a man
more certain of being engaged in the cause of
Christ. *The Lord at thy right hand shall strike
through kings in the day of His wrath. He shall
judge among the heathen ; He shall fill the places
with the dead bodies ; He shall wound the heads
over many countries. He shall drink of the
brook in the way ; therefore shall He lift up the
head.*[1]

Naturally to those who conceive the cause of
the Stuarts to be the cause of God, this attitude of

[1] Carl. iii. 5.

1650   Cromwell's must appear hypocritical or blasphemous. But such critics of history must surrender all hope of understanding Cromwell. The cause of the Stuarts was buttressed by deceits. It rested on a lie. The present king, who had taken the covenant, was a conscious and avowed hypocrite. And one must have a hatred of lies like Cromwell's own, to do him full justice. "Oh how good it is to close with Christ betimes," wrote the Captain-General from Alnwick on the march northwards, "there is nothing else worth the looking after. . . . Great place and business in the world is not worth the looking after; I should have no comfort in mine but that my hope is in the Lord's presence."[1] The Presbyterian ministers had filled the Scotch with terror. The English were "sectaries and blasphemers, who would put all the men to the sword and thrust hot irons through the women's breasts." That was a cruel libel. The fact was, this invading army was a church militant. The general theory in it was that "he who prays and preaches best will fight best." And a most favourable reaction was created when the country people found that any misconduct in the army was inexorably repressed by its own officers. War is a

[1] Carl. iii. 9.

stern business, and it is hard to think of it as Aet. 51
Christian at all. But if ever there was a Christian
army it was this which Cromwell led into Scotland,
to persuade, and if necessary to coerce, the misguided Presbyterian brethren. It consisted of
10,500 foot and 5500 horse, and it depended for
its supplies on the service of the fleet. It was
therefore essential to keep always in touch with
the coast. Leslie had at his command 26,000
men, but they were not the match of Cromwell's
veterans, and the ranks were divided by all the
divisions of Scottish parties, and weakened by the
constant interference of the Assembly of Presbyterian Divines.

For the whole of August 1650 the two armies
faced each other in different positions round Edinburgh ; and Leslie, by a Fabian policy, succeeded
in completely outmanœuvring his enemy. It
seemed as if Cromwell clung to the hope of con-
vincing the Scotch by argument. He wrote passionately to the "Honest people in Scotland."
"It is no part of our business," he says, "to
hinder any of them from worshipping God in that
way they are satisfied in their consciences by the
word of God they ought, though different from us,"
but that damning fact of "a king taken in by you

1650 to be imposed on us—and this to be called the
cause of God and the kingdom—a king that hath
a Popish army in Ireland, that hath Prince Rupert,
whose hand is deep in the blood of many innocent
men in England, in the head of our ships stolen
from us upon a malignant account . . . the depre-
dations on our coasts, strong combinations by the
malignants to raise armies in our bowels, by virtue
of his commissions," this it was which forced the
Commonwealth to call its Scottish neighbours and
friends to account.   And that lie of the king's
Covenant "so full of special pretences to piety,"
how could the Scotch be hoodwinked by it?
Surely their eyes might be opened.

   But argument could not avail.   Further, supplies were falling short, and sickness was reducing
the forces, as the season advanced, "beyond imagi-
nation."   At the end of the month, Cromwell was
compelled to draw back his army to its basis of
supplies on the coast, and Leslie triumphantly
hung on his rear, and occupied the heights above
Dunbar, while the parliamentarians barely succeeded in effecting their entrance into the town.
Here their supplies were secure; but the situation
was perilous and even desperate.   Dunbar is a
little seaport on a peninsula.   And Cromwell was

cooped up in a corner, the sea behind him and Aet. 51 Leslie's overwhelming forces in front. If ever he had entertained a doubt concerning his cause and its issue he must have lost heart at such a moment. Yet on September 2 he wrote to Haselrig at Newcastle: "All shall be for good. Our spirits are comfortable, praised be the Lord, though our present condition be as it is." It was a remark made by his friend Charles Harvey long afterwards: "He was a strong man; in the dark perils of war, in the high places of the field, hope shone in him like a pillar of fire when it had gone out in all the others." His correspondence admits us to the secret of this hope. He was entirely unembarrassed by private ends or personal fears. His work was his God's; and to doubt Him was not only sinful but impossible.

Conceive that little army, greatly reduced now, for 500 at least were in hospital, hemmed in by double their numbers entrenched along Doon Hill; the English on the lowland, the Scotch on the height, with the ravine of Cockburnspath between. The spirit of the Ironsides breathes in a soldier with a wooden arm, captured by the Scotch and brought before Leslie: asked if the enemy did intend to fight, he answered, "What do you think we come

1650 here for ? We come for nothing else." "But how
will you fight," asked Leslie, "when you have
shipped half your men and all your great guns?"
"Sir, if you please to draw down your men you
shall find both men and great guns too." How
durst he answer the General so saucily, asked the
officers. "I only answer the question put to me,"
replied the soldier, who was dismissed to the
English army to give them a sense of the hopeless
superiority of their enemies. All through the day,
on September 2, "the enemy drew down to the right
wing about two-thirds of their left wing of horse"
— we quote Cromwell's own account — " shog-
ging also their foot and train much to the right,
causing their right wing of horse to edge down
towards the sea. The major-general, Lambert, and
myself coming to the Earl Roxburgh's house, and
observing this posture, I told him I thought it did
give us an opportunity and advantage to attempt
upon the enemy. To which he immediately
replied that he had thought to have said the same
thing to me. So that it pleased the Lord to set
this apprehension upon both of our hearts at the
same instant. We called for General Monk and
showed him the thing; and coming to our quarters
at night, and demonstrating our apprehensions to

some of the colonels, they also cheerfully con-
curred." [1]

At four in the morning the moon shone out
of rainy clouds. The enemy's word was *The
Covenant*, the English *The Lord of Hosts*.
Lambert was to lead the attack on the enemy's
right. Cromwell with his own regiment and three
others was to turn the flank. As Hodgson was
speeding past in the night he caught the voice of
prayer rising from the lips of a cornet. "I met,"
he says in his *Memoirs*, "with so much of God in
it as I was satisfied deliverance was at hand." [2]
Soldiers and officers of this kind are difficult to
conquer.

There was some delay in Lambert's attack; but
by six o'clock Lambert's cavalry swept down upon
the Scotch, who were all unprepared. The infantry,
however, received a momentary repulse, but "my
own regiment," there to the left between the
Scotch and the sea, "did come seasonably in, and
at the push of pike did repel the stoutest regiment
the enemy had there, merely with the courage the
Lord was pleased to give, which proved a great
amazement to the residue of their foot." [3]   Just

---

[1] Cromwell's despatch of 11th September (Carl. iii. 45).
[2] Gardiner, *Commonwealth*, i. 324.   [3] Carl. iii. 44.

K

1650 then, through the morning mists, the sun appeared out of the eastern sea. Hodgson, who was near to Cromwell at the time, heard him say, " They run, I profess they run," and then, in the words of the Psalmist, " Let God arise, let his enemies be scattered ! "

Yes, the Scotch army, panic-stricken, was in full flight towards Haddington; many of the fugitives were turning aside to Dunbar, surrendering themselves as prisoners of war. " The Lord-General," says Hodgson, " made a halt and sang the 117th psalm "—the shortest and the gladdest of the psalms,—*His mercy is great toward us, and the truth of the Lord endureth for ever.* And then the horse swept on in pursuit.

The victory was complete. Three thousand of the Scotch were slain, and all their artillery, great and small, was in the hands of the victor. The English loss, the general believed, was not above thirty. The prisoners, 10,000 in number, were numerous enough to be an embarrassment. Cromwell sent 5000 of them to Haselrig at Newcastle with an entreaty that " humanity might be exercised towards them." [1] But in the forced march they died like flies. The survivors were

[1] Carl. v. 205.

sent to New England, where they were ultimately Aet. 51 set at liberty, and established as landowners in the settlement.

The general's mind was full of solemn reflections. "It is easy to say," he wrote next day, "the Lord hath done this. It would do you good to see and hear our poor foot to go up and down making their boast of God. . . . We that serve you beg of you not to own us—but God alone.[1]" If only we could have avoided bloodshed, for "God hath a people here fearing His name though deceived." And to his wife: "My weak faith hath been upheld. I have been in my inward man marvellously supported; though I assure thee I grow an old man, and feel infirmities of age marvellously stealing on me." He is thinking also of his other relatives, especially his son Richard, the wife and the child. "I pray tell Doll I do not forget her nor her little brat. She writes very cunningly and complimentally to me." A tender heart is never tenderer than on the morrow of a great battle and in the hour of gratitude for victory. To his son Ireton, too, he tells very movingly how he had sought "with sweet words and in sincerity" to win the Scotch.

[1] Carl. iii. 46.

1650 " We were rejected again and again, yet still we
begged them to believe we loved them as our
own souls." And lastly he writes, on that busy
September 4, to Lord Wharton, a waverer in the
cause, bidding him not to trust his own judgment.
For his own part he judges of " late transactions
by a better argument than *success*." [1]

As Naseby had rendered the establishment of a
purely personal government in England for ever
impossible, so Dunbar decided that the Solemn
League and Covenant should not impose its
tyrannical yoke on Englishmen. [2] In the first
battle Cromwell had been the champion of
political, in the second the vindicator of religious,
liberty.

But Charles, relieved from the durance of the
Covenanters, was in a more favourable position
than he had ever been to rally all parties in
Scotland to his support. And for a year, from
the fateful September 3 of 1650 to the fateful
September 3 of 1651, Cromwell was occupied in
the difficult endeavour to conciliate the stubborn
nation, and driven to the gradual conclusion that
another and a severer beating would still be
necessary before the business could be settled.

[1] Carl. iii. 56.   [2] Gard. *Commonwealth*, i. 329.

From Edinburgh he engaged in a lively controversy
with Presbyterianism. "We look on ministers as
helpers of, not lords over, God's people"; but the
Presbytery will admit no liberty, "any trying their
doctrines and dissenting shall incur the censure of
Sectary. And what is this but to deny Christians
their liberty and assume the infallible chair?"
Let the ministers preach by all means; but if
others receive the gift from Him who ascended up
on high, they also shall preach, and none shall
hinder.

The castle of Edinburgh held out under Dundas
until December 24. Cromwell's patience was extraordinary. He would even listen to preachers like
Mr. Zachary Boyd railing against him and his
army as sectaries and blasphemers.[1] Strachan
and Ker, who raised an army for the king in the
west, though on the understanding that he should
reform and be "subject to the King of kings,"
were treated so tenderly that after their decisive
defeat the former passed over to Cromwell. And
good news came to Edinburgh as the autumn
advanced. Blake was defeating Prince Rupert in
the Tagus, and the Commonwealth Admiralty was
forming a navy to repress the French and Royalist

[1] Carl. iii. 130.

1651 privateers, which, under Blake, Ayscue, and Penn
was soon to contend successfully with the Dutch
for the mastery of the seas. And two days
after Edinburgh Castle fell, Philip IV. of Spain
recognised the Commonwealth by sending Cardenas
as his ambassador to it, and presently dismissed
the Royalists, Cottington and Hyde, from Madrid.
On the whole Cromwell might exercise patience
towards the stiff-necked Scotch. But on January
1 they crowned Charles II. at Scone; and the
ministers reported that "he carried himself very
seriously and devoutly, so that none doubted of his
ingenuity and sincerity," for indeed he freely signed
both the National Covenant and the Solemn League
and Covenant.[1] That "Person in whom that which
is really malignancy and all malignants do centre,
against whose family the Lord hath so eminently
witnessed for blood-guiltiness,"[2] was crowned and
anointed king of Scotland. This iniquity would
not be ended by mercy or patience, but only by a
last and terrible drawing of the sword. Meanwhile
Cromwell was, on February 4, made Chancellor
of the University of Oxford. And on the same

---

[1] And yet "I am a true child of the Church of
England," he said to the Dean of Tuam; "Mr. King, I
am a true cavalier."   [2] Carl. iii. 78.

day an artist arrives to take his portrait for the Aet. 52
medal of Dunbar, the first medal of the kind given
to an English army, and Cromwell writes : " It will
be very thankfully acknowledged by me, if you will
spare the having my effigies in it." [1]

In March he exerted his influence to establish a
new university at Durham; for he had all the Puritan admiration of learning, and all a strong man's
zeal in promoting it.   And then for six months he
was very seriously ill with ague. The letters of that
time are very touching.   Many were written on
behalf of his opponents to the Speaker Lenthall; [2]
others to his beloved wife—" I love to write to my
dear, who is very much in my heart." Or he writes
to Richard Mayor about his son, who always causes
him some anxiety, "Truly I love him, he is dear
to me and so is his wife"; but Dick is one who,
to his father at least, seems to make " pleasure and
self-satisfaction the business of a man's life," a
view of things essentially incredible to a toiling
hero.[3]   It was at this period that Lady Stewart of
Allertoun, fervent Royalist as she was, had a passing
visit from the general, and afterwards affirmed
" she was sure Cromwell was one who feared God

[1] Carl. iii. 110.   [2] *Ibid.* v. 206-208.
                [3] *Ibid.* iii. 143.

1651 and had that fear in him, and the true interests of religion at heart,"[1] a fact about which there can now happily be no manner of question.

By the end of June 1651 Cromwell was sufficiently well to take the field against the new army which Charles had gathered round Stirling under the leadership of Leslie. The Scotch, rendered cautious by memories of Dunbar, were entrenched at Torwood, and Cromwell found it impossible to bring on an engagement. In July, therefore, he sent Major-General Lambert across the Forth to North Queensferry, with the intention of cutting off the supplies from Fife and so starving the enemy out of Torwood. Leslie sent his major-general, Sir John Brown, against Lambert, and at Inverkeithing, Lambert obtained a crushing victory, killing two thousand and capturing five or six hundred prisoners, Brown himself among them. This encouraged Cromwell to attempt one of the boldest feats of his life. He resolved to advance on Perth, with the clear foresight that the enemy, cut off from his northern supplies, would probably march into England. He felt it necessary to finish the campaign before winter, as his stores were low, and his men suffered from the climate.[2] Great

[1] Carl. iii. 132.   [2] *Ibid.* 141.

was the dismay in England; and some even
charged the general with treachery. But Cromwell's confidence was sublime : " Indeed," he wrote
on August 4, " we have this comfortable experience from the Lord that this enemy is heart-
smitten by God."

Harrison was sent forward to keep in check
the enemy's march, and Lambert was detached to
hang upon their rear. The last day of July the
Scotch marched away from Stirling, and on
August 6 Charles was at Carlisle. His hope in
marching through Lancashire and along the Welsh
border was to gather recruits. In this he was
disappointed. He stayed in the houses of Papists,
and alienated the Presbyterians. Lord Derby
came out to join his king, but was overthrown
at Wigan by Robert Lilburne on August 25.
Meanwhile Cromwell, leaving Monk in Scotland
to reduce Dundee, marched into England by the
more easterly road, supplying his commissariat in
his usual scrupulous way by buying in the markets
and paying ready money. On August 24 the
parliamentary generals united at Warwick. If
Charles had failed to gain recruits even by the
offer of a general pardon for all but regicides, the
militia, called out by the Council of State, crowded

1651 eagerly to Cromwell's banners. And when Charles marched into Worcester he had only 16,000 men to confront 30,000 of his enemies. It was September 3, Cromwell's fateful day. From the top of Worcester Cathedral Charles saw the bridge of boats thrown across the Severn and the Teme, and an attack threatened at St. John's gate on the south simultaneously with that on Fort Royal from the west. The battle was a foregone conclusion. But Cromwell was anxious to save his enemies. He "did exceedingly hazard himself, riding up and down in the midst of the fire, riding himself in person to the enemy's foot to offer them quarter, whereto they returned no answer but shot." Worcester was stormed, and the king driven in headlong flight from its walls. Writing at 10 P.M. that night, "being so weary and scarce able to write," Cromwell reported to Lenthall: "Indeed this hath been a very glorious mercy"—a crowning mercy, he called it next day—"and as stiff a contest for four or five hours as ever I have seen. Both your old forces and those now raised, have behaved themselves with very great courage, and He that made them come out made them willing to fight for you."[1]

[1] Carl. iii. 156.

It was the last battle that Cromwell fought, Aet. 52 and it was a crowning mercy in this sense, that the king's invasion of England at the head of a foreign army rallied all England to the parliamentary cause. For a moment at least the whole country turned with gratitude and love to its greatest man. His reception in London on September 12 was extraordinary: "In the midst of which," says Bulstrode Whitlocke, "my Lord-General carried himself with much affability; and now and afterwards in all his discourses about Worcester would seldom mention anything of himself; mentioned others only, and gave, as was due, the glory of the action unto God." This affability of the conqueror was on everybody's tongue. And when he reappeared in his place in Parliament on the 16th it was evident that he would spare no pains to realise a peaceful and stable settlement for a united country.

CHAPTER VIII

LORD PROTECTOR

1651–1653

> Yet much remains
> To conquer still ; peace hath her victories
> No less renowned than war : new foes arise,
> Threatening to bind our souls with secular chains ;
> Help us to save free conscience from the paw
> Of hireling wolves whose gospel is their maw.

THERE are some, like the Lilburnes and the Harrisons of his own day, who are well able to follow Cromwell with approbation up to a certain point in his career, but then comes a check. The strong, disinterested man seems suddenly to deflect into ambition and self-seeking. The Lilburnes gave him up when he maintained the divine authority of the army. The Harrisons gave him up, and then the Vanes gave him up, and finally all but a mere handful of discerning souls gave

him up, when he was driven step by step in the Aet. 52
discharge of his difficult task to assume powers
which, indifferent to him, were at the time essential for the settlement of the nation. With those
who, in spite of all the letters and speeches which
are before us, continue of the opinion that Cromwell was impelled from the first by personal
ambition, it is impossible to argue. Our business
is, not to defend him, but only to show that his
action, step by step, is perfectly consistent with
the other hypothesis, viz. that he acted under the
most constraining sense of duty to his country
and obedience to his God. No one will claim for
him infallibility. But absolute and transparent
sincerity, pathetic disinterestedness, and courageous
fearlessness of consequences in the discharge of
the day's task, are surely here, if ever they were
at all in the strong men who are called to
govern their fellows. "I am a poor weak creature,"
he writes on October 2 to his friend Mr.
Cotton, pastor of the church at Boston in New
England, "yet accepted to serve the Lord and
His people. Indeed, my dear friend, between
you and me, you know not me — my weaknesses,
my inordinate passions, my unskilfulness and
everyway unfitness to my work. Yet the Lord,

1651 who will have mercy on whom He will, does as
you see." [1]

From the crowning mercy of Worcester, September 3, 1651, to April 20, 1653, a period of
more than a year and a half, Cromwell was in the
background of events. And there is not the
slightest reason to doubt that he watched them
in the hope that a settlement would be reached
without his intervention. He had done his part
at Naseby, Dunbar, and Worcester. The enemies
of the Commonwealth were prostrated. Now let
Parliament and the Council of State do the rest.
He was the servant of these authorities and had
no design to be their master. No doubt he was
anxious when Parliament, now in its eleventh
year, a mere remnant after its repeated purges,
scornfully called in the country the Rump, showed
no readiness to dissolve and make way for a true
representative assembly. But he acquiesced for
the moment in the decision that the dissolution
should take place in three years time, on November 3, 1654, and when the fourth Council of
State was appointed on November 24, 1651, he
cheerfully consented to act as their president.

In November Ireton, the brave doctrinaire, the

[1] Carl. iii. 173.

devout and loyal Christian, died, and Cromwell, Aet. 52
writing to his sister-in-law at Ely on December
15, says: "I have herewith sent you twenty
pounds as a small token of my love. I hope I
shall be mindful of you. I wish you and I may
have our rest and satisfaction where all saints
have theirs. What is of this world will be found
transitory; a clear evidence whereof is my son
Ireton's death."[1] In July Fleetwood was sent to
Ireland to take Ireton's place; he also married
Ireton's widow, and so became Cromwell's son-in-
law. A letter to this new son-in-law, written
apparently soon after the appointment, shows us
in what channel the thoughts of Cromwell were
running—not exactly the channel of personal
ambition: "The new Covenant is grace. . . . This
commends the love of God: it's Christ dying for
men *without* strength, for men whilst sinners,
whilst enemies. And shall we seek for the root
of our comforts within us. What God hath done,
what He is to us in Christ, is the root of our
comfort: in this is stability; in us is weakness.
Acts of obedience are not perfect, and therefore
yield not perfect grace. Faith as an act yields it
not, but as it carries us into Him, who is our

[1] Carl. v. 214.

1652 perfect rest and peace, in whom we are accounted
of, and received by, the Father, even as Christ
Himself. This is our high calling. Rest we here
and here only." [1]

It is not psychologically conceivable that this
should be the tenor of his private correspondence
with his intimates while he was, as history (save
the mark !) has represented him, secretly plotting
his own aggrandisement. During the year 1652
Parliament was debating the question of law-
reform, a matter of vital moment in Cromwell's
opinion, who described the English law codes as
"a tortuous and ungodly jumble." [2] Bulstrode
Whitlocke was the mover of the proposition.
But the moribund "Rump" had not the vitality
to attack so great a question. Indeed the
paralysis at the centre of government was daily
becoming more perilous. And yet it seemed
equally perilous to dissolve and to appeal to the
uncertainties of a general election ; for the
Commonwealth was at war with the Portuguese,

[1] Carl. iii. 190.
[2] There were 23,000 unheard cases waiting in
Chancery. The Civil War had shattered the whole
system of feudal tenure ; and the very basis of a settlement, security of property, awaited a drastic reform of
the law.

" whereby our trade ceased; the evil consequences Aet. 53 by that war were manifest and very considerable. And not only this, but we had a war with Holland; consuming our treasure, occasioning a vast burden upon the people"—this was the war arising out of the Navigation Act, which ended by Blake and Monk wresting from Van Tromp and de Ruyter the naval supremacy of Europe,—" A war which cost this nation full as much as the taxes come unto, the navy being a hundred and sixty ships, which cost this nation above £100,000 a month. . . . At the same time also we were in a war with France;" trade was hindered "by reason of the advantages taken by other states to improve their own, and spoil our manufacture of cloth, and hinder the vent thereof—which is the great staple commodity of this nation."[1] Evidently complications of this kind could only be met by a strong executive, or by a parliament representing a united nation; nay, let us admit that of the two the executive was the more necessary.

On August 13 Cromwell received a petition from the officers, demanding some real reform of the law, a gospel ministry, and a prompt end to the Rump Parliament. This led to a series of

[1] Speech ii. Carl. iv. 32.

1653 meetings between the officers and the members of Parliament. "We had at least ten or twelve meetings most humbly begging and beseeching of them that by their own means they would bring forth those good things which had been promised and expected; that so it may appear they did not do them by any suggestion from the army, but from their own ingenuity, so tender were we to preserve them in the reputation of the people." [1] In the last of these conferences, which took place on April 19, 1653, the House of Commons could only muster fifty-three members. To this had the great Parliament of 1640 dwindled. It could pretend to no popular sympathy or support. And yet it dared not dissolve. After all it was the only phantom of constitutional government which survived after the prolonged convulsions. The throne had gone; the Lords had gone; and the Commons, reduced and violently purged, a little junto of fifty-three, stood alone as the governing authority of a great nation. It had not the courage to resign; that would seem to throw the nation into the seething-pot. It could only consent to a new Parliament on condition that the existing members of the old were to be *de jure* members of the new,

[1] Carl. iii. 208, Speech i.

and were to constitute a committee with the Aet. 54
powers of deciding which of their successors should
sit ! This was indeed an impotent conclusion.
A great nation, engaged with powerful foes at
home and abroad, waiting to be reconstituted
and governed; a discredited remnant of a bygone
Parliament, powerless to govern, powerless to
cease to be ! How was this feeble and dangerous
obstruction, which legally had the sole right of
dissolving in its own hands, to be removed?
Another eighteen months of this futility and weakness might be the ruin of the cause for which the
army had fought, and in which Cromwell had seen
at every step the decisive manifestations of the
divine approval.

Cromwell had as deep-rooted a love of consti-
tutionalism as any man; but here there was no constitutional method possible. He had a still greater
love of his country and his cause. And this was
his peculiar merit, that, in humble dependence
on God, he dared to strike out a new path where the
paths of the constitution had been obliterated
or blocked. On April 20, 1653, after earnest consultation with his officers,—" the thinking of an act
of violence was to us worse than any battle that ever
we were in, or that could be to the utmost hazard

1653 of our lives; so willing were we, even very tender and desirous, if possible, that these men might quit their places with honour,"—he stepped over to the House, took his seat, and after listening for awhile, "perceiving the spirit of God so strong upon me, I would no longer consult flesh and blood,"[1] he bade the members go. They must give place to better men. His musketeers under Harrison were there to enforce the decision. Thus the Long Parliament was dispersed, Cromwell telling Vane that he might have prevented it if he would, "The Lord deliver me from thee, Sir Harry Vane."

We possess a letter, written three days after this forceful action, to the adventurers who were engaged in draining the great level of the Fens. Cromwell, with the instinct of the governor who can attend to small, while he is apparently occupied in great things, despatches a troop of his cavalry to repress certain rioters who were interfering with the works, "who may by all means persuade the people to quiet, by letting them know they must not riotously do anything, for that must not be suffered; but if there be any wrong done by the adventurers, upon complaint,

[1] Carl. iii. 196.

such course shall be taken as appertains to Aet. 54
justice, and right will be done." That was the
spirit of this *usurper*. He had usurped power,
and entered upon a most toilsome and perilous
course, that his country might be saved, and a
firm government established. It was part of his
sacrifice for his country and his God, that he
quietly faced the odious imputation of usurper and
tyrant, because there was no other way by which
the Commonwealth could be saved. His course
of action is transparent as the day, his motives are
perfectly unmistakable, if we are only content to
study his words to the Convention, which he and the
Council took immediate steps for calling together.

This Assembly, a convention of notables
rather than a Parliament, and nicknamed by
Royalist wits Barebones Parliament, because a
worthy leather-merchant from the city, named
Praise Barbone, chanced to sit in it, was of course
in the constitutional sense not a parliament at all.
There was no king to issue the writs; the three
estates of the realm were for the moment obliterated; and an appeal to the constituencies must
have resulted in a House which would immediately
reopen all the questions raised in the Civil Wars.
It was therefore with a solemn and even awful

1653   sense of responsibility that " I, Oliver Cromwell, Captain-General and Commander-in-Chief of all the armies and forces raised and to be raised within this Commonwealth, with the advice of my council of officers," summoned these 140 persons, "fearing God, and of approved fidelity and honesty," as representative of the counties and boroughs, to appear at Whitehall on July 4, 1653. An analysis of the names shows that these nominees of Cromwell were the best men that England at the moment possessed. Rouse, the Provost of Eton, was Speaker; and the rest were types of that great religious, God-fearing party in England which had triumphed over a despotic throne, and punished the Church as its abettor. The fault of this remarkable assembly was that, with no ambition to govern, but with a strong desire to make England Christian, it pursued a course which alienated all the godless and the lukewarm elements in the kingdom, and then in less than five months, on December 2, very readily handed up its powers, which it never sought, to the Lord-General who had conferred them. All that it attempted was noble; its ideas were a prophecy of the course which English reforms would follow in the next three centuries; what it accomplished was nothing. It is gibbeted in Aet. 54 history, as unrealised ideals too frequently have been, by those frivolous and futile people who realise their ideals, because their ideals are of the earth, earthy.

But the great speech which Cromwell delivered to this ephemeral assembly is the complete explanation, if not the vindication, of his action in dissolving the Rump, and in assuming, as he was now logically forced to assume, the sovereign power. He pointed to the extraordinary dispensations of God during these past twelve years—" those very great appearances of God, in crossing and thwarting the purposes of men, that he might raise up a poor and contemptible company of men, neither versed in military affairs, nor having much natural propensity to them, simply by their owning a principle of godliness and religion."   Before this "poor and contemptible company" the throne and the Church had gone down; it had been carried victoriously from point to point; Catholic Ireland, Presbyterian Scotland, had been broken in resisting it.   Now it was at the helm of State, responsible for the settlement of the country. "The gloriousness of the work may well be attributed to God Himself, and may be called His

1653 strange work. . . . I say there is not any one of
these things," up to "His marvellous salvation
wrought at Worcester, but hath an evident print
of Providence set upon it, so that he who runs
may read." Thus being imperatively summoned
by God to the task he had undertaken, he had
ventured to dissolve the old Parliament because it
was doing nothing, and hindering the necessary
settlement, but determined "not to grasp at the
power ourselves, or keep it in military hands, no
not for a day; but as far as God enabled us, with
strength and ability, to put it into the hands
of proper persons that might be called from the
several parts of the nation." He had called the
present assembly together, from "this necessity,
and I hope we may say for ourselves this integrity
of concluding to divest the sword of all power in
the civil administration."

And now these men, among whom he had
not allowed himself "the choice of one person in
whom we had not this good hope, that there was
in him faith in Jesus Christ and love to all his
people and saints," must seek the wisdom which
is from above; for the affairs of this nation were
now in their hands—the cause of Christ depended
upon them. He concluded by saying that he had

"within a week set up a Council of State" as an Aet. 54 executive, "eight or nine of them being members of the House that late was."

Certainly it was all open to grave misconstruction, and the world until recently has agreed to misconstrue it, but the intention and conscience of the main actor need not be misunderstood. "I am in my temptation ready to say," he wrote to his son Fleetwood a month later, "Oh would I had wings like a dove, but this I fear is my haste. I bless the Lord I have somewhat keeps me alive, some sparks of the light of His countenance and some sincerity above man's judgment." [1]

The failure of this Convention was a bitter disappointment to Cromwell. In it was heard that melancholy voice of fanaticism which follows so easily on a deep religious movement. Major-General Harrison and the Fifth Monarchy men would abolish the ministry, close the law courts, disband the forces, and expect the personal reign of Jesus. All this was fatal to the desired settlement. And when the assembly proffered its resignation, Cromwell sorrowfully and yet willingly accepted it. Some other way must be found.

The ferment of this fanaticism was as dangerous

[1] Carl. iii. 234.

1653   as Royalist plots, and far more formidable than the Dutch and Portuguese wars. If ever in the history of England a strong hand was needed it was now. If ever a strong hand, divinely strengthened, was at England's disposal, it was Cromwell's. On December 2 the Convention Parliament resigned ; for a few days the Lord-General was in constant and prayerful conference with his Council of Officers and others who were tried and trusted ; on December 16 the announcement that Cromwell had accepted the title of LORD PROTECTOR OF THE COMMONWEALTH OF ENGLAND, SCOTLAND, AND IRELAND, was solemnly confirmed by a stately installation in Westminster Hall. " His Highness was in a rich but plain suit, black velvet with cloak of the same ; about his hat a broad band of gold." An instrument of government appointed a council of twenty-one, and defined in forty-two sober articles the lines of the Constitution.

This was the usurpation of Oliver Cromwell. From this moment to September 3, 1658, somewhat under five years, he was virtually the sovereign of England. If one asked him, by whose authority, he would doubtless answer " God's." He was not chosen by the nation, nor by a parliament. The council which carried

through the transaction was a council of his own Aet. 54
appointment. He did not rest his title on this
flimsy foundation. For himself he was convinced
that God, by His dispensations, had called him to
a distasteful and difficult task. He meant to
carry it through. The reason why he would not
allow any one to question his title, was that he
regarded it as given him by God. The reason
why his vindications of himself sound to us
laboured and involved is that it is impossible by
words, and barely possible by acts, to make good
a claim to an inward call of God.

CHAPTER IX

GOVERNMENT AT HOME AND ABROAD

1653–1658

" Our business is to speak things. . . . Jesus Christ, of whose diocese they and you are."—CROMWELL.

IT is not denied that Oliver was a usurper, and in the old Greek sense of the word, a tyrant. But the remarkable fact is that he was impelled to his perilous and arduous course of action by duty and not by ambition; and his government was the most disinterested, the strongest, the most enlightened, the hopefullest, that England had ever seen. Nay, as if by inspiration, this usurping Protector proceeded to shape ideals for the progress and influence of his country, which, dissolved for the moment by the blessed Restoration, have remained as the aim of our political development ever since. Part of Oliver's splendid—surely God-

given—ideals are now realised in England, and Aet. 55
they make her the most fortunate country in
Europe; part remain still unfulfilled, and they
furnish to ardent and patriotic souls the goal of
aspiration and endeavour.

In February 1654 the city received the Protector in royal style; approbation and encouragement began to pour in from different parts of
England, Yorkshire especially distinguishing itself
by a vote of the grand jury at the County General
Assizes, which was a great comfort to His Highness.
The judges, after consultation, determined to receive
their commissions from him, and the justices of the
peace at once acknowledged his authority. More
striking still, the chief courts of Europe sent their
congratulations as to a sovereign. And it is
probable that Milton, who was the Latin secretary
of the new council, Thurloe being the ordinary
secretary, expressed the very general feeling of
moderate men when he maintained that the new
office was a necessity, and urged Oliver to carry into
its duties the resolution and the Christian zeal which
he had manifested in the other positions he had
filled.

By a show of hands it is quite possible that
England would have been against the Government;

1654 but by an estimate of sober and responsible heads, the heart and conscience of the country were with it. Of course the Royalists were in opposition, and never ceased to hatch their plots, encouraged by the Royal Proclamation which now appeared : " Whereas a certain base mechanic fellow, by name Oliver Cromwell, has usurped our throne," whosoever will kill him " by sword, pistol, or poison " shall be rewarded with money and promotion " on the word of a Christian king." Unhappily, too, the Republicans of the army, and the Fifth Monarchy men throughout the country—strong men, like Ludlow, Bradshaw, Hutchinson, Sydney, Haselrig, and Vane, and weak men, of the Lilburne type— could not forgive the usurper. They had fought not against the abuse, but against the existence of the throne, and now here was the throne re-established. Its justice, its mercy, its efficiency, could never reconcile them to it. In their eyes it was an iniquity from the beginning. There are always the Cato's, the Brutus's and Cassius's, strong, honest souls, who, firm in great ideals, would prefer chaos to a government which contravenes their principles. What gave to Cromwell his peculiar strength and raised him to his unique position, was that he had no abstract theories of government ;

he was no doctrinaire; he had no fads to realise. Aet. 55
His ideal was justice, firm government, and above
all a thoroughly Christian administration. With
his eye steadily fixed on that end, he could freely
work for it with the instruments and by the
methods which came ready to his hand. The
world owes most to its great dreamers; a country
and a generation owes most to its practical men.
In the long run to be an idealist is the one way of
being practicable; but for the day's work it is
often the way of being impracticable.

A Parliament was summoned for September 3,
1654. But during the nine intervening months,
Oliver and his council worked with a vigour and
effect which seem literally supernatural. Abroad,
peace was immediately concluded with the Portuguese and the Dutch; and the grand conception
was formed of a Protestant Alliance with Sweden,
Denmark, and Holland. And meanwhile, as an
example to Europe of British justice, Dom Panta-
leon Sa, the brother of the Portuguese Ambassador,
was publicly beheaded for his share in the murder
of an English citizen. Indeed it was the first
effect of the Protectorate to give to England a
consideration in Europe which she had never
secured before and has seldom enjoyed since.

1654   At home, during these nine months, eighty-two ordinances were issued, dealing with almost every part of the social organisation. A reform of the Court of Chancery, which the Convention Parliament had gallantly undertaken, was swiftly carried through. But the most characteristic piece of work was the method for appointing and maintaining a pure and devout ministry throughout the country. To Oliver this was essential. His opposition to Rome and to Episcopacy arose entirely from his desire for a more direct, personal, and spiritual religion. Accordingly, by the Ordinance of March 20, 1654, a commission of thirty-eight was nominated for the trial of public preachers. Nine were laymen, with Francis Rouse, Provost of Eton, at their head. The rest were ministers of very different ecclesiastical views, Presbyterian, Independent, even Anabaptist. They included Owen, Goodwin, Manton. But all were agreed in the view that ministers must be godly men who were commissioned by God, and not merely by the universities. Even so learned a man as Thomas Fuller found it difficult to pass the test of the Triers, as they were called, and two years later besought John Howe, Cromwell's household chaplain, to help him through the difficult ordeal.

By another Ordinance in August commissioners Aet. 55
were appointed, from fifteen to thirty, in each
county to deal with " scandalous, ignorant, and
insufficient " ministers, who were to be ejected,
with a modicum of maintenance if they had wives.
In 1656 Oliver could appeal to the conscience of
his Parliament, " Whether or no there hath not
been an honest care taken for the ejecting of
scandalous ministers, and for the bringing in of
them that have passed an approbation; I daresay
such an approbation as never passed in England
before. And give me leave to say, it hath been
with this difference that neither Mr. Parson nor
doctor in the University, hath been reckoned
stamp enough by those that made these appro-
bations, though I can say too they have a great
esteem for learning . . . so this ministry was
never so upon the thriving hand since England
was, as at this day." [1] He hoped much from this
arrangement, and in all his speeches to Parliament
referred to it as one of the most satisfactory
features in his government. It was the first and
last attempt ever made by a State Church to
appoint men to the ministry, not on the ground of
certain ecclesiastical opinions, or articles of a

[1] Carl. iv. 208.

M

1654 creed, but solely for spiritual fitness and on evidence of a real conversion to God and faith in our Lord Jesus Christ. And no State Church can attempt it again, because never again can there be an absolute ruler of England who is conscious of being a deputy of Jesus Christ.

In the summer came Vowel and Gerard's plot to assassinate the Protector; but the Government was on the alert. Five of the conspirators were seized in their beds. On this occasion the Latin Secretary was told to write to Cardinal Mazarin explaining the expulsion of M. De Baas from England for some connection with the plot; and the letter finely illustrates the strong and independent tone which the Government could assume towards France.[1] And indeed negotiations for a treaty with France were on foot. The powers of Europe desired to be on friendly terms with the master of the fleet which swept the seas.

Altogether when the new Parliament, 400 in number, assembled in September 1654 Oliver had all those signs of blessing on his government which he was sure to interpret as the divine approbation. He was prepared to cordially welcome his " loyal and trusty " Commons, and to

[1] Carl. v. 224.

establish them in their office and administration. Aet. 55
But on one point he was perfectly clear, he would
not allow them to question or even to discuss the
authority which God had put into his hand, and
he had already exercised with eminent success, for
more than nine months.   He was determined to
stand firm on the Written Constitution—the first
of the kind the world had seen, the instrument of
government by a single person and a parliament.

On Monday September 4 Parliament assembled.
Thomas Goodwin preached the sermon in the
Abbey,[1] "His Highness seated over against the
pulpit, the members of the Parliament on both
sides"; and then all adjourned to the Painted
Chamber, where "His Highness put off his hat
and made a large and subtle speech to them."
The speech recounts with a dignified humility the
successes of the Government, lays bare the perils
occasioned by the Levellers, and their disturbances
even in the army, and assures the honourable members that they "are met on the greatest occasion
that I believe England ever saw; having upon your
shoulders the interests of three great nations with
the territories belonging to them; and truly I
believe I may say it without any hyperbole, you

[1] Bulstrode Whitlocke's report (Carl. iv. 19).

1654 have upon your shoulders the interest of all the Christian people in the world."

There could be no possible question about the light in which Oliver regarded the duties of government.

But unhappily the Parliament, having chosen Lenthall as its Speaker, began by deliberating whether they should approve the newly established frame of government. There were returned among many solid Constitutionalists some convinced Republicans, like Bradshaw, Haselrig, and Scott. Avowed Royalists were not eligible. But impracticable Republicans would do the work of Royalism. The discussion was protracted over some days; it might easily go on for ever. From the constitutional standpoint nothing could be weaker than this government; from the Republican standpoint nothing could be more criminal. While such a fundamental discussion proceeded, how was the Government to be carried on? If it resulted in disapproval and condemnation—then, there was chaos come again.

On the morning of September 12 the Protector summoned his Parliament to the Painted Chamber, and for an hour and a half pleaded with them to avert the disaster by frankly recognising the

constitution and proceeding to the pressing Aet. 55
practical duties of the hour. He asked them to
bear with him if he a little magnified his office,
for his one thought had always been, if God will
not bear it up, let it sink. God and the people,
God as the Agent, the people by their acquiescence,
he averred, had made him Protector; the calling
was from God, the testimony from the people;
none but these august authorities should displace
him. He told them with touching earnestness,
God being his witness between him and all men,
that he would have preferred to retire into private
life. But God by His providence had commanded;
he had not shrunk and would not. He accepted
this high office. " I was arbitrary in power, having
the armies in the three nations under my command;
and truly not very ill-beloved by them, nor very
ill-beloved by the people, by the good people. . . .
All the people in England are my witnesses; and
many in Ireland and Scotland. All the sheriffs in
England are my witnesses; and all that have come
in upon a process issued out by sheriffs," viz. :
these honourable members "are my witnesses."
The hereditary interest of the old throne was
surely no better confirmation than this distinct
decision of Providence. He stood between

1654 England and anarchy. God had settled certain
fundamentals which might not be called in
question; the first was, that the Government
should be by a single person and a parliament;
and he was the single person. That parliaments
should not make themselves perpetual; liberty of
conscience in religion; the right management of
the militia; these were fundamentals. "The
wilful throwing away of this government, such as
it is, so owned by God, so approved by men, so
witnessed to in the fundamentals of it as was
mentioned above, and in reference to the good of
these nations and of posterity; I can sooner be
willing to be rolled into my grave and buried with
infamy, than I can give my consent unto." [1]

In one word, the Parliament House was closed
and would not be open to any who would not sign a
declaration admitting the government under which
the members had been summoned. "The instrument of government doth declare that you have a
legislative power without a negative from me . . .
you may make any laws, and if I give not my
consent within twenty days to the passing of your
laws, they are *ipso facto* laws, . . . if not contrary
to the frame of government." That is all that is

[1] Carl. iv. 65.

required.   It was the strong voice of a man, commissioned like an ancient prophet to accomplish a
stern task, determined not to be baulked by mere
pedantries.   The times were out of joint, and he
was born to put them right.   At all costs, even at
the risk of being maligned as a tyrant, he meant
to do his work.

In the course of the month 300 of the members
signed the declaration.   Republicans like Bradshaw, Haselrig, and Scott, would not sign but
withdrew.   Major Wildman, a violent Anabaptist,
retired to prepare a "declaration of the free and
well-affected people in England now in arms
against the tyrant Oliver Cromwell," but in
February he was arrested and shut up in Chepstow
Castle.

His Parliament thus purged, the Protector
communicated to the Speaker Lenthall a design
by sea, which he was maturing, for the welfare of
the Commonwealth in the West Indies; and other
letters show his eager desire to have the hearty
co-operation of his Parliament in his far-reaching
plans of government.   A week later we hear of
him making a small picnic under the trees in Hyde
Park with Secretary Thurloe, and trying some
horses which had been sent him from the Duke of

1655 Oldenburg. He was thrown and dragged by the
foot some way, and a pistol went off in his pocket.
But it is a relief to find that the burdened mind
had its moments of relaxation. He was making
" England more formidable and considerable to all
nations than ever it has been in my days," wrote
a correspondent from the Continent. He was also
living in daily fear of assassination from misguided
Englishmen, and therefore carried a pistol. His
mother, who died at the age of ninety-four in
November, with the blessings of a lifetime upon
him—" My dear son, I leave my heart with thee :
a good-night ! "—had lived in daily apprehensions
of his being shot, could not bear to hear a
gun, and had insisted on seeing him every day to
satisfy herself that he was alive.[1]

Adjutant-General Allen, another Anabaptist,
was stirring disaffection in the West. On January
20, 1655, Cromwell writes to Exeter with orders
to keep a watch on him. Two days later he
dissolved his Parliament. He explained his
reasons in a long and passionate speech. " As I
may not take notice what you have been doing, so
I think I have a very great liberty to tell you that
I do not know what you have been doing " . . .

[1] Carl. iv. 73.

and later, " you have wholly elapsed your time, and Aet. 56
done just nothing ! " Meanwhile, plots have been
thickening, hatched by Anabaptists in the army, and
by " that cavalier party " throughout the country.
" For myself, I desire not to keep my place in this
Government an hour longer than I may preserve
England in its just rights, and may protect the people
of God in a just liberty of their consciences." But
while men are trying to debauch and divide our
armies, Parliament has not taken the trouble to pro-
vide for the pay, which is thirty weeks in arrear. In
Scotland the men have been incited to seize their
general, Monk, and to put Overton at their head,
and to march into England on the plea of their
arrears. Never a word has the Parliament
addressed to him, the Protector, on the pressing
questions of the day. It had passed its time in
discussing abstract questions; for practical purposes in a time of disorganisation and difficulty it
was useless. " I can say," he told them, " that no
particular interest, either of myself, estate, honour,
or family, are or have been prevalent with me to
this undertaking." If they had proposed that the
government should have been placed in his family
hereditarily, he would have rejected it. " This
hath been my principle; and I liked it when this

1655 government came first to be proposed to me, that it puts us off that hereditary way." [1]

In a word, he had been placed there, and guided in his government, by the most unmistakable dispensations of God; to deny the divine hand in it seemed to him to be blasphemy. But his Parliament had made no honest attempt to help him in his appointed task. It had not even voted supplies, but left him to raise money according to the article in the government. "I think myself bound," therefore, "as in my duty to God, and to the people of these nations for their safety and good in every respect, . . . to tell you that it is not for the profit of these nations, nor for common and public good for you to continue here any longer. And therefore I do declare unto you that I do dissolve this Parliament."

[1] Carl. iv. 100.

CHAPTER X

RULER, BUT NOT KING

"Pulcherrimi facti laus atque gloria illibata atque integra tua erit."—MILTON.

FROM January 22, 1655, to September 17, 1656, Cromwell carried on the government without a parliament, in the hope that he might bring things into order, and pave the way for a parliament which would help and not hinder his work. His speech in dismissing his Parliament makes two things perfectly clear, first, that he had no intention of usurping the throne, but had in his mind a magistracy, not hereditary, which would be under the authority of the people; and second, that while he was magistrate he was determined to rule firmly, justly, and in the fear of God.

The months of February and March were mainly occupied in suppressing Anabaptist and Royalist plots. Wildman, as we saw, was

1655 imprisoned. Penruddock and Grove, who at Salisbury seized the judges in their beds and proclaimed King Charles, were run to earth, condemned at the Assizes, and beheaded, while many of their supporters were hanged or sold as servants in the Barbadoes. Oliver writes to the authorities at Gloucester and Worcester urging them to nip these dangerous designs in the bud, and indeed proves, as he always did, that in vigilance and promptness of action, he was a born ruler of men. Speaking on the assembling of his second Parliament he recounts these events. "The insurrection was intended first to the assassination of my person, which I would not remember as anything at all considerable to myself or you" . . . "an officer was engaged, who was upon the guard, to seize me in my bed." But what was more serious was this, that the plotters had sent a wild fanatic, Sexby, to the court of Madrid, to the enemies of religion and of England, "to advise with the king of Spain to land forces to invade the nation." It was this almost incredible delusion of the Republican and Anabaptist fanatics, the delusion that even Charles Stuart would be better than Oliver Cromwell, the delusion that the cause of liberty and of England could be served by a

Spanish invasion, which stimulated Oliver's fiery purpose to maintain his government against all opposition.

As Parliament was for the time being out of the question, he found out what he calls " a little poor invention " for preserving order, and crushing the attempts of Levellers and Royalists. The country was divided into ten districts towards the end of May; and over each district was placed a major-general, supported by the militia, with well-nigh absolute powers. There was to be no appeal except to the Protector in Council. On all Royalists who were disaffected the major-generals imposed a tax of ten per cent, known as the decimation. We cannot wonder that an outcry was raised against this dangerous innovation; but it is an extraordinary testimony to the integrity of these Commonwealth men,—Desborow, Skippon, Fleetwood, Whalley, were amongst the best known names—that the arrangement worked to the satisfaction of all unbiassed minds. The Government was arbitrary, but it was unflinchingly just. With all its dangerous possibilities, the actual nominees of Cromwell to this arduous duty were men against whom even malice could not wag a tongue.

1655   In these months, too, the Protector attacked in his resolute way the abuses of the Court of Chancery, that "tortuous and ungodly jumble." In spite of the outcry from Widdrington and Whitlocke, who resigned their legal posts, he actually effected, by an Ordinance in Council, some definite reforms of that dilatory and costly court. His eye also was on the Criminal Law. "There is one general grievance," he said in 1656; "it is the law. Not that the laws are a grievance; but there are laws that are. . . . I think I may say it, I have as eminent judges in this land as the nation has had these many years . . . but, there are wicked and abominable laws. To hang a man for 6s. 8d., and I know not what; to hang for a trifle, and acquit murder,—is in the ministration of the law, through the ill-framing of it. I have known in my experience abominable murderers acquitted; and to see men lose their lives for petty matters—this is a thing God will reckon for." [1]

This was highly characteristic of Cromwell. There was hardly a flaw in our constitution, in law or practice, which his keen eye did not detect; and his vigorous hand, arbitrary as it was, struck out the lines along which reform was to move. If one

[1] Carl. iv. 209.

looked at the foundation of his government, even Aet. 56
friends might cavil; from the nature of the case
it was absolutely unconstitutional. If one looked
at the procedure and achievements of his government, even foes were silenced. "His greatness at
home," wrote Clarendon, "was but a shadow of
the glory he had abroad." Such disinterested
righteousness has never, before or since, been
manifested in the conduct of affairs. And it was
on this that Cromwell's own eyes were fixed; for
this, he believed, he would render account.

Nor was it only at home that the strong just
hand was felt. It was in his relations with the
courts of Europe that his genius as a ruler became
most conspicuous. Papal Spain was necessarily a
foe, and he determined to humble her. With
France on the other hand he wished to live in
peace. Cardinal Mazarin feared Oliver more than
the devil, it was said. When, in the middle of 1655,
Oliver was about to sign a treaty of peace with
the government of Louis XIV., there came to
London the news of a shocking massacre which
had been perpetrated in the Savoy Alps by the
Duke of Savoy. His subjects there were Protestants. A true son of the Church, he sent friars to
convert them. But, unhappily, one of the friars

1655 was assassinated. Forgetting every principle of Christianity, the Duke despatched six regiments of soldiers to offer them conversion or violent expulsion from their hereditary valleys. The mandate was carried out with violence and bloodshed. When, on June 3, the event of the preceding winter was reported at Whitehall, it moved Oliver to tears, and Milton to a sonnet, which breathes the very spirit of the English Commonwealth—

> Avenge, O Lord, Thy slaughtered saints, whose bones
> Lie scattered on the Alpine mountains cold.

Oliver refused to sign the treaty with France unless she would protect the persecuted Piedmontese. He wrote to the Duke, to Mazarin, to Louis XIV. by Secretary Milton, to the kings of Sweden and Denmark, to the States-General, to the Swiss Cantons, to the prince of Transylvania, fully determined that, if his appeals had been unsuccessful, he would have drawn the sword of England in defence of these unhappy Christians. But it was not necessary to engage in war. The voice of Oliver rang through Europe, and strong nations trembled. England raised a sum of £100,000 for the unhappy refugees.[1]

[1] "The Papacy, and those that are upholders of it, they have openly and avowedly trodden God's people

During this summer Blake was busy in the Aet. 56
Mediterranean. The Duke of Tuscany, the Pope,
the Deys of Tunis, Tripoli, and Algiers, in succession were forced to make reparation for injuries
done to English commerce and liberty. The
Mediterranean was cleared of pirates. "By such
means as these," said the Protector, "we shall
make the name of Englishman as great as that of
Roman was in Rome's most palmy days."[1] It is
charming to observe that on the same day that he
wrote to his admiral his directions for the design
of intercepting the Spanish Fleet, June 13, the
Protector wrote to the poet Waller to thank him
for his *Panegyric to my Lord Protector*. "Indeed
I am passionately affected with it. I have no
guilt upon me unless it be to be revenged for your
so willingly mistaking me in your verses."[2] And
a week later comes one of those beautiful domestic

under foot, on this very motive and account that they were
Protestants. The money you parted with in that noble
charity which was exercised in this nation, and the just
sense you had of those poor Piedmonts was satisfaction
enough to yourselves of this, that if all the Protestants of
Europe had had but that head, that head had been cut off
and so an end of the whole" (Cromwell's Speech xvii.,
Carl. v. 105).

[1] *Encycl. Brit.* 9th edit. vol. vi. 603.
[2] Carl. v. 231.

N

1655 letters which constantly remind us that the loving and devout Christian was never lost in the great man of affairs and the ruler of England. It is addressed to his son-in-law, Fleetwood, Lord Deputy of Ireland, and refers to his son Henry who was to succeed Fleetwood in the Irish government. But for the present the affectionate father says that there was no thought of replacing the one by the other. "The noise of my being crowned, etc., are similar malicious figments. . . . Dear Charles, my dear love to thee, to my dear Biddy (*i.e.* Bridget, his wife) who is a joy to my heart for what I hear of the Lord in her. Bid her be cheerful and rejoice. . . . We, under all our sins and infirmities, can daily offer a perfect Christ; and thus we have peace and safety, and apprehension of love, from a Father in covenant, who cannot deny Himself. And truly in this is all my salvation; and this helps me to bear my great burdens." [1] He had no wish, perhaps no need, to be crowned. "I have not the particular shining bauble for crowds to gaze at or kneel to," he wrote to Secretary Thurloe, "but whatever I think proper for outward form to refer to any officer, I expect that such my compliance with custom

[1] Carl. iv. 126.

shall be looked upon as an indicative of my will Aet. 56
and pleasure to have the thing *done*." The inner
consciousness of a divine call had given him a
kingly bearing. His dealings with ambassadors
were marked by "a carriage full of gravity and
state." How he carried himself to the humblest
servants of God, George Fox has left on record.
Fox had an interview with him in his bed-
chamber, and as he left to give place to some
great man, "He caught me by the hand and
with moist, beaming eyes, said, 'Come again to
my house. If thou and I were but an hour
together, we should be nearer one to the other.
I wish no more harm to thee than I do to my
own soul.'"

The expedition to the West Indies was not a
success, though Jamaica was occupied. "I pray
you set up your banners in the name of Christ,"
wrote Oliver to his admiral there, "for undoubtedly it is His cause." In October 1655 war
with Spain was formally declared. "We think,
and it is much designed among us," wrote Oliver
to Jamaica, "to strive with the Spaniard for the
mastery of all those seas, . . . and that a very
special regard may be had so to govern, for
time to come, as that all manner of vice may

1656 be thoroughly discountenanced and severely punished."

In the spring of 1656, and on into the summer, the Protector was in constant correspondence with his "Generals Blake and Montague at sea." The directions given them are practical and explicit enough; but the foundation of all is an assurance of this kind: "You have, as I verily believe and am persuaded, a plentiful stock of prayers going for you daily, sent up by the soberest and most approved ministers and Christians in this nation; and notwithstanding some discouragements, very much wrestling of faith for you, which is to us, and I trust will be to you, matter of great encouragement." The same tone pervades his letters to his son Henry: "If the Lord did not sustain me I were undone; but I live and I shall live to the good pleasure of His grace; I find mercy at need. The God of all grace keep you." Probably no government was ever fortified with so much prayer. If the men of the Commonwealth had an excellence which is peculiar to the period; if Sir Matthew Hale adorned the bench; if Blake and the great sea captains set England in the front of the world as a naval power; if great theologians like Owen

and Goodwin, and Cudworth, adorned the Aet. 57
universities; if efficient secretaries like Thurloe
and Milton were available for the Government
departments; it is easy to see that a constant
habit of prayer was the explanation of this general
efficiency. This was an atmosphere in which
good men were encouraged, and good men
became great.

Certainly it was not from any sense of need,
but purely from a determination to fulfil the provisions of the Instrument, that another Parliament
was summoned to meet on September 17, 1656.
Of the four hundred members elected, one
hundred,—chiefly violent Republicans, like Haselrig
and Scott, but other turbulent spirits like Ashley
Cooper,—were not allowed to sit. The time had
not yet come when the Government could be
exposed to the violent dissensions and the untiring
attacks of men who would not accept the general
principle of government vested in a single person
and Parliament. Such a sifting of the members
was, from a constitutional point of view, in-
defensible. But with that point of view Oliver
had no concern. His one purpose was that the
country should be ruled in the most efficient way.
"Rhetoricians I do not pretend to; neither with

1656 them nor what they use to deal in, words. Truly *our* business is to speak things." And confining himself to *things*, it was indeed a noble and a proud record which he was able to give to the new members, fresh from Vice-Chancellor Owen's sermon, on the text: *What shall one then answer to the messengers of the nation?* (Isaiah xiv. 32). There was war with Spain, true. Spain is a natural enemy, a kind of anti-Christ with which Christ must inevitably be at war. To ask from that country's ambassador liberty of conscience or satisfaction for injuries was " to ask his master's two eyes." With such a nation one ought to be at war. And in that war God was blessing England; for even about the time of this reassembling of Parliament, Blake and Montague had captured a Spanish fleet. Eight-and-thirty waggon loads of silver came up from Portsmouth to the Mint.[1] But, " I say we are at peace with all other nations." Unhappily the Papists in

---

[1] " Never was there a more terrible visible hand of God in judgment upon any people," wrote the papers, " since the time of Sodom and Gomorrah. Great is the Lord and marvellous are His doings and to be had in reverence of all the nations." This refers to the earthquake at Lima which occurred during this summer and buried still more of the Spanish king's silver (Carl. iv. 224.)

England are "Spaniolised."   The Spaniard also Aet. 57
"hath espoused Charles Stuart."   But while English Papists and Spanish enemies are abetting
the cavaliers, "there are a company of poor men
that are ready to spend their blood against such
compliance."   The major-generals have been completely successful in crushing Overton, Wildman,
Penruddock, and the rest, though Sexby is still at
large.   Religious liberty has been secured: " I
would not be willing to see the day when England
should be in the power of the Presbytery to
impose upon the consciences of others that
profess faith in Christ."   The tithes were maintained, and scandalous ministers had been ejected.
Profaneness, disorder, and wickedness had been
discouraged, nay even repressed.   "The mind is
the man.   If that be kept pure, a man signifies
somewhat; if not I would very fain see what
difference there is betwixt him and a beast."   He
could solemnly protest that he did not know of
one action in his government, however apparently
unconstitutional, which had not been "in order to
the peace and safety of this nation."   As for his
own conscience he is very clear: "I am by the
voice of the people the supreme magistrate.   It
is a union between you and me, and both of us

1656 united in faith and love to Jesus Christ and to
His peculiar interest in the world, that must
ground this work. And if I have any peculiar
interest personal to myself, which is not subservient
to the public end, it were not extravagant of me
to *curse* myself; because I know God will curse
me if I have. I have learned too much of God to
dally with Him, and to be bold with Him in these
things." [1]

The new Parliament abolished the major-generals
and the system of "decimating" the property of
Royalist recusants. It was also occupied with the
case of a Quaker fanatic, James Nayler, who had
scandalised Bristol by entering the town with some
women singing Hosannah to him; and this brought
from the Protector a letter to the Speaker in which,
while expressing abhorrence of the man's proceedings, he desires that the House will let *him* know
the course it is taking." [2]   He speaks in the plural
of royalty. The day after, he wrote a royal letter to
Mazarin; cordial "as your brother and confederate,"
but firmly for the present refusing the toleration
to Catholics for which the Cardinal had asked.

Indeed, it was no time to relax the rigour of the
Government towards its relentless internal enemies.

[1] Carl. iv. 217.   [2] *Ibid.* 242.

On January 8, 1657, it was Thursday, as the even- Aet. 58
ing service was proceeding in the Protector's chapel
at Whitehall, an old quartermaster named Sindercomb was seen loitering suspiciously "near the
Lord Lambert's seat." . . . At eleven o'clock
that night the sentry found a lighted fuse attached
to a basket full of combustibles. About midnight
the Palace would be in a blaze. Oliver was
awakened, and the Council was summoned. Two
guardsmen were sent to Sindercomb's lodging to
arrest him. It was one of the unceasing plots of
the Levellers, working in collusion with the
Royalists abroad. Sexby's book, *Killing no
Murder*, which encouraged the assassination of
the Protector, had borne such fruit in the attempt
of his confederate. Sindercomb poisoned himself
in the Tower. Parliament went over to congratu-
late their sovereign on his escape. He acknowledged their solicitude in a grateful speech which
touched on the many mercies God had shown to
the nation, and especially "the most growing
blessing," of a gospel ministry, "such an one as
hath excelled itself." And he added : "You
have a good eye,[1] and in that I will share
with your good favours; a good God, a God

---

[1] Carl. iv. 236 —"I will guide thee with mine eye."

1657 that hath watched over you and us; a God that hath visited these nations with a stretched-out arm."

It was this perpetual restlessness of Royalist and Leveller plots, together with the unmistakable power and fitness of Oliver for the regal office, that now turned the attention of Parliament to a plan for settling the constitution on a firmer basis. On February 23, 1657, Sir Christopher Pack moved a remonstrance to His Highness which proposed a second Chamber, and increased powers to the single person in the Government. Four days later Oliver received a deputation of a hundred officers, who were dismayed at the project for making his Highness king, which would be hazardous for him, a scandal to God's people, and a step towards the return of Charles Stuart. Oliver showed in his reply that he had no wish for the title, "a feather in the hat," but that their schemes hitherto had not succeeded in settling the nation as desired, and it was possible that a return to the ancient constitutional forms would lead to such a settlement. Accordingly during the spring, while he was engaged in negotiating the new treaty with France, by which Dunkirk would come into English hands (March 23), and while Blake

was gaining another famous victory over the
Spaniards at Santa Cruz (April 20), and on to
the decisive answer (May 8), a perpetual discussion was maintained in Parliament, and repeated
conferences were held between Parliament and
Oliver, whether he should be crowned or no.
Eight of the speeches delivered on that subject
are before us, and they are a luminous revelation,
not only of his mental conflict on this particular
question, but also of his settled thoughts and fully
developed character. " I have lived the latter
part of my age in—if I may say so—the fire ; in
the midst of troubles.[1] . . . Give me time to ask
counsel of God and of my own heart.[2] . . . That
may be fit for you to offer, which it may not be fit
for me to undertake.[3] . . . I am not able for such
a trust and charge.[3] . . . I do not find it my duty
to God and you to undertake it under that title.[4]
. . . Great places, great authority, are a great
burden. I know it so. And I know a man that
is convinced in his conscience, nothing less will
enable him to the discharge of it than assistance
from above. And it may very well require in
such a one, so convinced and so persuaded,

---

[1] Carl. iv. 247.   [2] *Ibid.* 249.   [3] *Ibid.* 252.
[4] *Ibid.* 253.

1657 that he be right with the Lord in such an undertaking." [1]

The day after these last words were uttered,
April 9, a cooper named Venner headed another
Fifth Monarchy rising at Mile-End; but the ringleaders were lodged in the Tower. The discussion
and the entreaties went on. But, "I must say I
should be a person very unworthy of such favour
if I should prevaricate in saying things did stick
upon my conscience. Which I must still say they
do.[2] . . . The laws may still be executed as
justly without such a title as with it.[3] . . . And
truly I may say that almost universal obedience
hath been given by all ranks and sorts of men to
the Protectorate.[4] . . . I do not think there hath
ever been a freer procedure of the laws.[5] . . . I
undertook my place, not so much out of hope of
doing any good, as out of a desire to prevent
mischief and evil—imminent evil . . . comparing
myself to a good constable set to keep the peace
of the parish. . . . I judge for myself there is no
necessity for this name of king.[6] . . . It would
grieve godly men in this nation, who have been

---

[1] Carl. iv. 256.   [2] April 11, Carl. iv. 270.
[3] Carl. v. 4.   [4] *Ibid.* v. 7.   [5] *Ibid.* v. 8.
[6] *Ibid.* v. 10, 11.

faithful and have bled all along in this cause.[1] . . . Aet. 58
Truly the Providence of God hath laid aside this
title of king *de facto*. . . . He hath not only
eradicated a whole family but the name or title.[2]
. . . I do not think the thing necessary; I do not.
I would not that you should lose a friend for it.[3]
. . . I have not desired the continuance of my
power or place either under one title or another,
but I thank God I know where to lay the weight
that is laid upon me, I mean the weight of reproach
and contempt and scorn that hath been cast upon
me.[4] . . . The things that are provided for in this
Act of Government do secure the liberties of the
people of God so as they never before had them.
Liberty *de jure* from God I think they have had
from the beginning of the world to this day, and
have it still, but asserted by a *jus humanum* I say
they never had it so as they have it now. I think
you have provided for the liberty of the people of
God and of the nation. And I say he sings
sweetly that sings a song of reconciliation betwixt
those two interests.[5] Yes, the Instrument in every
other respect is good. The reformation of manners,

[1] Carl. v. 15.   [2] April 13, Carl. v. 17.
[3] *Ibid.* v. 19.   [4] April 20, Carl. v. 26.
            [5] *Ibid.* v. 46.

1657 excellent; the trial of ministers,—if they have the root of the matter in them, they may be admitted, be they Presbyterian, Independent, or Baptist— just what it should be. I speak in the fear and reverence of God.[1] The revenue must be increased, but that is a trifle.[2] . . . As to the title of king, however, every man who is to give an account to God of his actions must in some measure be able to prove his own work and to have an approbation in his own conscience; if I took the title, at the best I should do it doubtingly. And certainly whatsoever is so is not of faith. I cannot undertake this government with the title of king."[3]

Thus the question was settled. There was to be a second Chamber. The Lord Protector was to exercise the duties of kingship,—might even nominate his successor,—but king he would not be. On May 25 he accepted this newly-defined authority. "I came hither," he said to Parliament, "not as to a triumph, but with the most serious thoughts that ever I had in my life, to undertake one of the greatest tasks that ever was laid upon the back of a human creature." Nor would

[1] Carl. v. 67.   [2] April 21, Carl. v. 66.
[3] May 8, Carl. v. 71.

he have undertaken " this insupportable burden to Aet. 58
flesh and blood" if he had not seen proofs of his
Parliament's cordial support. On June 26 came
the great installation in Westminster Hall, stately
and solemn as a coronation. The Speaker in the
name of Parliament delivered to him a robe of
purple velvet, a Bible richly gilt and bossed, a
sword, and a sceptre of massy gold. Then the
Lord Protector took the oath, and chaplain Manton
offered prayer. Afterwards the people gave several
great shouts and the trumpets sounded. England
and Europe recognised Oliver as king in all but
name.

CHAPTER XI

THE WORK ACCOMPLISHED

1657–1658

" The world is built on the dust of heroes."—CARLYLE.

1657 FOR fifteen months Oliver reigned with all the dignity and consideration of a king. On July 3 he resigned his post as Chancellor of Oxford, finding other duties more than sufficient for his strength. In September his foreign policy was marked by a great success. Montague captured Mardike; and in the following June Dunkirk became an English garrison, only to be forfeited at the glorious Restoration. The despatches written to Montague and Lockhart on this matter are almost the last of Oliver's letters which have come down to us, those strong, nervous, intensely pious letters, which reveal the man whom we have been studying with photographic clearness. In

October, one stormy element at least was removed
from the Protector's life by the arrest, and death
in prison, of the Anabaptist Sexby. The plots
were not altogether to cease, nor were the troubles
of Parliament to be entirely overcome. It was
storm and trouble to the last. But a certain calm
and consolation as of an approaching port begin to
pervade the atmosphere. In November he had
the satisfaction of seeing his two youngest daughters
suitably married, Frances to Robert Rich, grandson
of the Earl of Warwick; Mary to Lord Faucon-
berg. The attempt to prepare for a permanent
settlement by the new Instrument of government
involved two very dangerous elements. It was no
longer possible to exclude the irreconcilables,
Haselrig, Scott, Ashley Cooper and the rest.
They must be allowed to sit if they chose to take
the oath. . . . And there was the new House of
Lords. Sixty-three members were summoned to
it, the tried soldiers of the war, Skippon, Desborow,
Whalley, Prior, Hewson—who had started life as
a shoemaker—Whitlocke, Haselrig, Lenthall,
Rouse, and other old Commoners, and six of the
old peerage, of whom only Lord Eure actually
took his seat. Oliver was bent on trying this new
constitution, and bravely faced its manifold perils.

o

1658 He met Parliament on January 20, 1658, with a
speech, firm and cheerful, which was a sermon on
the text, " Mercy and truth are met together :
righteousness and peace have kissed each other."
Nathaniel Fiennes followed with a discourse in a
similar vein, comparing the state of England to
cosmos emerging from chaos, the two firma-
ments being the two Houses of Parliament.

But alas ! the restored members began at once
to raise the whole question of the Constitution,
and to proclaim their implacable objection to the
single person.   And this, at a moment when the
Pope and the Catholic powers were designing an
attack on England ; when the Duke of Ormond
was in London in disguise ; and Charles, with his
four Irish regiments, hoped to cross the channel in
twenty-two ships hired from the Dutch, supported
by a Spanish army of six or even ten thousand !
The situation was made immediately intolerable.
On the 25th the Protector called the members
together and pleaded passionately with them.   All
might go well if only the impracticable party
could be awakened to a sense of the danger.
Here was their army unpaid, " the soldiers going
barefoot at this time, in this city, this weather ! "
If the army in Ireland were not paid, it would

come on the settlers for free quarter, and break Aet. 59
them.   All the toil and bloodshed there would be
thrown away.   " I beseech God touch your hearts
and open your ears to this truth, and that you
may be as deaf adders to stop your ears to all
dissension. . . . Indeed if we turn again to folly
let every man consider if it be not like turning to
destruction. . . . I sought not this place.   I speak
it before God, angels, and men ; I did not.   You
sought me for it, you brought me to it.   I took my
oath to be faithful to this government, that every
just interest may be preserved, that a godly
ministry may be upheld, and not affronted by
seducing and seduced spirits ; that all men may
be preserved in their just rights, whether civil or
spiritual."   It was all in vain.   The pedants and
doctrinaires would not be silenced ; but proceeded,
while the forces of invasion were marshalling themselves across the sea, not to pay and equip the army,
but to settle whether the Protector should be continued in his present position.   It was infatuation ;
it was even madness.   It was no time to raise the
question of either the single person, or the second
Chamber ; the state of England demanded prompt
and united action.   On February 4 the Protector
again summoned the Parliament to his presence,

1658 and delivered the last speech which has come
down to us. It was very earnest and very brief.
He would have gladly avoided his onerous and
difficult post; he would have preferred to have
lived under his woodside, to have kept a flock of
sheep. "You advised me to come into this place,
to be in a capacity by your advice. Yet instead
of owning a thing, some must have I know not
what; and you have not only disjointed yourselves
but the whole nation, which is in likelihood of
running into more confusion in these fifteen or
sixteen days that you have sat, than it hath been
from the rising of the last session unto this day."[1]
The intemperate agitators were stirring the army
to revolt while "the king of Scots hath an army
at the waterside ready to be shipped for England."
In a word, "I do dissolve this Parliament, and let
God be judge between you and me."

This peremptory step was taken only just in
time; "if their session had continued but two or
three days longer all had been in blood both
in city and country upon Charles Stuart's account." Despatches were sent into the counties
explaining the position, and the common sense
of the country recognised the necessity of the

[1] Carl. v. 129.

step.   " Having done nothing," so ran the despatch, " in fourteen days but debate whether they
should own the government of these nations as
it is contained in the *Petition and Advice* which
the Parliament in their former sitting had invited
us to accept of and had sworn us unto ; they
themselves having taken oath upon it before they
went into the House," [1] and we judging this
dangerous for the nation and despairing of getting
supplies, from such men as are not satisfied with
the foundation we stand on, thought it absolutely
inevitable to dismiss the Parliament and to take
affairs into our own hands again.   And it is
observable that immediately the whole threatened
rising was suppressed, and Ormond went back to
his king to report that there was no hope while
Oliver held the reins of power. Sir Henry
Slingsby and Rev. Dr. Heriot were brought before
a high court of justice for their share in this
abortive rising. They were beheaded on Tower
Hill, June 8.   While the trial proceeded Oliver
was writing to Lockhart, the ambassador at the
French Court, on behalf of " the poor people of
Piedmont professing the reformed religion," with
" fresh arguments of pity towards them, not only

[1] Carl. v. 241.

1658 as men, but as the poor distressed members of Christ." His plan was that the French king should exchange some equivalent of territory with the Duke of Savoy and bring these valleys under his more enlightened government. To the last, as long as Oliver was free to act, unhampered by the carping and questioning of the pedants in Parliament, his voice was the most potent voice which England had ever raised in the courts of Europe; anarchy at home and invasion from abroad were immediately rendered impossible.

But here was the melancholy fact. With all his splendid efficiency, and all his incorruptible justice, he was not destined to propitiate the favour of Levellers or Royalists, nor to reconcile the power which he used so well with the rights of a free parliament. That part of his task he was to leave unfinished ; and as that was the keystone of the arch, the whole constitution was to crumble away. He was to leave behind him not a secure and stable Commonwealth, governed by an elective Protector and a popular Parliament, but only the splendid vision of a firm, an enlightened, a Christian administration, to which, during his brief years of power, he had given body and form. Only six months of life remained, "He being

compelled," wrote a contemporary,[1] "to wrestle
with the difficulties of his place, so well as he
could, without parliamentary assistance, in it met
with so great a burden as (I doubt not to say) it
drank up his spirits, of which his natural constitution yielded a vast stock, and brought him to
his grave; his interment being the seed-time of
his glory, and England's calamity." The strong,
great soul, so freely offered in life for his country
and his God, was to be literally yielded up in
death, faithful to that twofold service. "His
body was well built," says the same witness in
words partly quoted before, "compact and strong,
his stature under six feet (I believe about two
inches), his head so shaped as you might see in it
a storehouse and shop both of a vast treasury of
natural parts. His temper, exceedingly fiery, as I
have known, but the flame of it kept down for the
most part or soon allayed with those moral
endowments he had. He was naturally compas-
sionate towards objects in distress, even to an
effeminate measure," this stern, invincible soldier;
"though God had made him a heart wherein was
left little room for any fear, but what was due to

[1] Letter from Maidston to Winthrop, governor of
Connecticut (Thurloe, i. 763).

1658 Himself, of which there was a large proportion,
yet did he exceed in tenderness towards sufferers.
A larger soul, I think, hath seldom dwelt in a
house of clay than his was." A capacious, genial,
lovable man, although his business in this world
was stern and uncompromising. Take this little
picture, which Bulstrode Whitlocke has preserved
from the time of the debates concerning the
kingship : " He often advised about this or other
great businesses with the Lord Broghill, Pierpoint,
Whitlocke, Sir Charles Wolseley, and Thurloe,
and would be shut up three or four hours together
in private discourse, and none were admitted to
come to him. He would sometimes be very
cheerful with them, and, laying aside his greatness,
he would be exceedingly familiar; and by way of
diversion would make verses with them, and every
one must try his fancy. He commonly called for
tobacco, pipes, and a candle, and would now and
then take tobacco himself. Then he would fall
again to his serious and great business." [1]

The most human of men, tender, passionate in
his tenderness, who would have preferred to live
" under his own woodside," cherishing wife and
children, loved by rustic neighbours ; but driven to

[1] Carl. iv. 272.

" tread the paths of glory, and to sound the depths Aet. 59
and shoals of honour" by no choice of ambition
but by the stern voice of God.   A great ruler of
men, but greater as a father, a citizen, a Christian
than as a ruler.   A man who lifted the star of
England from the murky shadows of tyranny and
national degradation, in which it had set, to the
zenith ; a man whose heart would break over the
loss of a daughter whom he loved.   On February
16 Mr. Rich, the young husband of Frances, died.
Oliver wrote to his grandfather, the Earl of
Warwick, letters so "seasonable and sympathising,"
says the recipient,—" which, besides the value they
derive from so worthy a hand, express such
faithful affections, and administer such Christian
advices as renders them beyond measure dear to
me,"—that he could not sufficiently confess, much
less discharge, his obligation.   But in July the
Protector was called to face a sorrow which no
human words could comfort.   His beloved
daughter, Elizabeth Claypole, lay ill at Hampton
Court, with a painful, depressing, and incurable
disease.   All public business was laid aside.   The
governor of a great country became merely an
anxious, prayerful father.   For a fortnight he
watched her unceasingly.   He loved her, every

1658 one loved her, but he loved her beyond his life. He himself sickened in the strain of this terrible anxiety. Harvey, watching him day by day, saw his strength decline, "a most indulgent and tender father," who shone in that and all other personal relations "a most rare and singular example;" and indeed he wondered how the burdened mind and body had sustained the stress of life so long "except that he was borne up by a supernatural power." On Friday, August 6, Elizabeth died; and with her the heart of her father died. A few days after, confined to his room, he asked for his Bible and read the passage, "I have learned in whatsoever state I am therewith to be content. . . . I can do all things, through Christ which strengtheneth me." Turning to Harvey he said, "This Scripture did once save my life, when my eldest son (Robert) died,[1] which went as a dagger to my heart, indeed it did." Paul had learned that lesson, and as he revolved the words his faith rose triumphant. "He that was Paul's Christ is my Christ too." During these days of August George Fox came to Hampton Court, to plead for the Friends, and in his strange inspired way "saw and felt a waft of death go forth against

[1] In 1639, *see* Carl. i. 41.

him." The illness, a "bastard tertian" grew upon Aet. 59
him, and he was ordered to return to Whitehall,
in the hope that the air would be better in London
than on the river. It was now generally known
throughout the country that his life was in danger,
and "prayers abundantly and incessantly poured
out on his behalf, both publicly and privately, as
was observed, in a more than ordinary way." This
praying people even cherished hopes that he would
be restored, and for a time he himself inclined to
the same thought, but "we could not be more
desirous he should abide," says Harvey, "than he
was content and willing to be gone."

As he lay dying his mind was absorbed in the
Covenant, that gracious guarantee of salvation
which God has made with man, and sealed in Christ.
"Faith in the Covenant is my only support," he
murmured, "and if I believe not He abides faithful. . . . Is there none that will come and praise
God, whose mercies endure for ever ? . . . Children,
live like Christians; I leave you the Covenant to
feed upon." His spirit rose up in triumph. "The
Lord hath filled me with as much assurance of His
pardon and His love as my soul can hold. . . . I
think I am the poorest wretch that lives; but I
love God, or rather am beloved by God. . . . I

1658 am a conqueror, and more than a conqueror,
through Christ that strengtheneth me." Intrepid
victor of Naseby, Dunbar, and Worcester, van-
quisher of a tyrannical throne and of a persecuting
Church, he is not in these last glad, solemn hours
thinking of these passing victories; his thought is
in the eternal things, and in that supreme
conquest of sin and death, the work of Christ
Jesus his Lord, of which he by faith had been
made a partaker.

On Monday, August 30, raged that tempest
which seemed to every observer the fitting dirge
of the earth over the passing of a noble soul;
and in the height of the storm he murmured a
prayer which was fortunately taken down by
Harvey.

"Lord, though I am a miserable and wretched
creature, I am in a covenant with Thee through
grace. And I may, I will, come to Thee for Thy
people. Thou hast made me, though very unworthy, a mean instrument to do them some good
and Thee service; and many of them have set too
high a value upon me, though others wish and
would be glad of my death; Lord, however thou
may dispose of me, continue and go on to do good
for them. Give them consistency of judgment,

one heart, and mutual love; and go on to deliver Aet. 59 them, and with the work of reformation; and make the name of Christ glorious in the world. Teach those who look too much on Thy instruments to depend more on Thyself. Pardon such as desire to trample upon the dust of a poor worm, for they are Thy people too. And pardon the folly of this short prayer, even for Jesus Christ's sake. And give us a good night if it be Thy pleasure."

On Thursday, September 2, Harvey watched with him through the night and heard him frequently say with much cheerfulness and fervour of spirit, " God is good." He would be willing to live and serve God and His people further. " But my work is done. God will be with His people." He was urged to take a potion and to try to sleep. " It is not my design," he answered, " to drink or sleep; but my design is to make what haste I can to be gone."

September 3 was the glorious thanksgiving day for Dunbar and the crowning mercy of Worcester. The victor lay calm and speechless, and between three and four in the afternoon he was dead.

The grand life was over, a firm, consistent act of faith, a brave fight for righteousness, justice and mercy, a simple, humble, Christian life.

1658   Cromwell's work was done. He had shattered the throne which threatened the liberties of England, and the Church which was incapable of admitting the rights of conscience. When the throne was restored, as it shortly was, it rested on a parliamentary basis, and was thenceforth to be limited by the people's will. When the Church was restored, it attempted for twenty-eight years to carry out its former ruthless policy, but the Commonwealth had sown the imperishable seeds which issued in the Act of Toleration and the modern general confession that no state has the right or the power to coerce the conscience of men. Before the eyes of persecuting prelates rises the awful form of Cromwell as a warning and a terror. This was Cromwell's work; it was done, efficiently and finally; under the Great Taskmaster's eye the task was carried to its legitimate end.

But how much more he accomplished, as it were incidentally ! He united Scotland and England, and gave to the northern kingdom her first start in a glorious career of progress. He drew the lines of the Reform Bill of 1832 ! He began the noble work of reforming English law. He foreshadowed the consideration which England

might hold in the counsels of the world if only 1658
she could be rid of Stuarts and all their ways.
And not the least, though alas! but a transitory,
service was his practical administration.   We are
still striving to secure an administration as firm,
as just, as incorruptible as the Protector's, and to
maintain a court as pure.   The administrative
machinery was for seven years absolutely honest,
disinterested, and sound.   There were no official
abuses, no waste, no peculation.   The whole power
of the State was used on the side of sobriety,
purity, cleanness of life and tongue.   For the first
and only time in Europe morality and religion
were the sole qualification insisted on by a court.
Cromwell was the first ruler of England whose
service no vicious man might enter.

There was not heroism enough in England to
maintain such a government.   The indispensable condition—another Cromwell, as the single
person of the Government—was lacking.   But if
England knew the day of her visitation and the
things which make for her peace, she would raise
the statue of Cromwell, not only in Manchester
where the sole statue of Cromwell at present
stands, but in every free and busy town, and she
would write the principles of his administration on

the minds of all her children. And at least she
must in simple gratitude admit that the best
things she to-day enjoys, the dearest liberties and
the brightest hopes, she owes to that sternly-tender
workman of God, Oliver Cromwell.

THE END